# Peterloo

*A 200th anniversary reprint of*

# The Story of Peterloo

## Written for The Centenary: 16 August 1919

by F.A. Bruton

# The Mask of Anarchy

by Percy Bysshe Shelley

Annotated for the 200th anniversary edition
by George Cavendish

Solis Press

*The Story of Peterloo* by F.A. Bruton was first published in 1919.

*The Mask of Anarchy* by Percy Bysshe Shelley was first published in 1832 (written in 1819).

The maps on pages 53 and 54 were first published in *Three Accounts of Peterloo* edited by F.A. Bruton in 1921.


*Acknowledgements*
Cover: detail from "Manchester Heroes" by Robert Cruikshank, Library of Congress Prints and Photographs Division Washington, D.C. 20540, USA. http://hdl.loc.gov/loc.pnp/pp.print
Page 56: image of Percy Shelley, Carl H. Pforzheimer Collection of Shelley and His Circle, The New York Public Library. (1848–1905). Percy Bysshe Shelley, from the original picture by Clint. Retrieved from http://digitalcollections.nypl.org/items/c4ce8f13-712d-d3e6-e040-e00a180664e5

This edition published by Solis Press, 2019

ISBN: 978-1-910146-40-8

Published by Solis Press, PO Box 482,
Tunbridge Wells TN2 9QT, Kent, England
*Web*: www.solispress.com | *Twitter*: @SolisPress

# Contents

## *Illustrations*

## *Maps*

❦

## *The Mask of Anarchy*

# The Story of Peterloo: The Site

OF THE THOUSANDS OF people who stream out of the Central Station every day, perhaps it does not occur to many that as they descend the gentle slope in front of the station they have immediately before them the site of Peterloo.[1] The street that runs parallel to the front of the station immediately outside the gates is Windmill Street; Windmill Street is cut at right angles by three other streets—Watson Street on the left, Mount Street in the centre, and Lower Mosley Street on the extreme right. All four of these streets were in existence at the time of the tragedy of the 16th of August, 1819, though the houses in Windmill Street and Mount Street ran along one side only. Parallel to Windmill Street, and on the other side of four great blocks of buildings, runs Peter Street, now one of the main arteries of the city. With the exception of a fragment at the Deansgate end, Peter Street hardly existed at the date of Peterloo, except as a projected causeway across an open space.

Perhaps the best spot from which to obtain a general conception of the scene is the top of South Street. If we stand to-day at the point where South Street cuts Windmill Street, and look northwards down towards Peter Street, we have immediately on our left the south-eastern corner of the Free Trade Hall.[2] Apparently it was just within the site of that corner that the two carts stood that formed the hustings for the great meeting. If we now imagine that the three blocks right and left of us—the Free Trade Hall and the Tivoli Theatre on the left, and the Theatre Royal and the Y.M.C.A. on the right, are swept away, and the whole space cleared, from Windmill Street on the south right back to the Friends' Meeting House on the north, and from Watson Street on the west to Mount Street on the east, we shall have before us the open space known in 1819 as St. Peter's fields, where the great meeting was held. St. Peter's church, built in 1794 (the site is now marked by a stone cross) stood in the open to the north-east. The whole space now occupied by the Midland Hotel was then a high-walled garden, in which stood a residence known as Cooper's cottage; at the south-western corner of this enclosure, where we now see the Buffet of the Midland, stood a row of some half-dozen houses, facing Mount Street, in one of

---

1 Peterloo was named, in an ironic sense, after the 1815 Battle of Waterloo.

2 Built 1853–6, this was to commemorate the repeal of the Corn Laws in 1846. The hall was built by public subscription. The building still stands and at present is a Radisson Hotel.

which—the residence of Mr. Buxton—the magistrates assembled on the eventful day. From this house a double cordon of some hundreds of special constables[3] reached as far as the hustings, which we have already located. The troops employed were concealed at some little distance from the area, in the side streets; one body being accommodated in Pickford's yard, off Portland Street.

The streets of Manchester, if we will only see them aright, are thronged with the memories of nearly two thousand years; of the many epoch-making events that have been associated with them, few, if any, have sent such a thrill through the country as the tragedy which took place in the area we have just defined on the 16th of August, 1819, when there assembled here what proved to be the most important of all the many meetings in favour of Reform[4] which were held in the early part of the nineteenth century.

The slight sketch which follows is an attempt to give as vivid, accurate, and impartial an account of this event as may be possible after the lapse of a hundred years. In order to do that intelligibly, it will be necessary to name a few of the sources from which information is obtainable.

---

3 Civilians retained by the police. Generally unpaid but they have powers of arrest.

4 In this sense the reform of Parliament, e.g. better representation and a wider franchise.

# Authorities for the Details of Peterloo

THOUGH NO MONOGRAPH ON the tragedy of Peterloo has appeared so far, the literature dealing with the subject is considerable. We turn first of all, naturally, to the periodical publications of the day—the local newspapers, of which there were five, the London and provincial press, and the monthly and quarterly magazines. Of the five local papers, all weekly, two favoured the "Reformers," as the agitators among the working classes were called at the time; the other three were more or less antagonistic to them. For a proper understanding of the occurrences of the day it is advisable to follow the issues of these papers for many months, indeed for several years, before and after the event; one of the trials, for example, took place nearly three years after the catastrophe.

It is a curious and interesting fact that the future editors of two Manchester newspapers not then founded, both of whom were present in St. Peter's fields on the 16th of August, 1819, finding that the reporter for the London *Times*[5] had been arrested at the hustings, and fearing that therefore the accounts in the London papers would be one-sided, unfairly condoning the action of the magistrates, determined to send a report to London themselves, which duly appeared in two leading London papers. These two men were John Edward Taylor, the founder and first editor of the *Manchester Guardian*, and Archibald Prentice, founder and first editor of the *Manchester Times*. Taylor, who was in business at the time, immediately constituted himself the protagonist among the champions of the "Reformers," and opened the battle in a series of fourteen weekly tracts entitled "The Peterloo Massacre," the first of which appeared just a week after the event. His clear reasoning and strong democratic leanings are visible in a number of other protests which appeared at the time; the flame of his indignation against anything that savoured of tyranny seemed only to burn more brightly in the face of adverse verdicts; and when, less than two years later, the assistance of a number of friends made it possible for him to issue the prospectus of the *Manchester Guardian*, foreshadowing a newspaper that should aim at "fixing on a broader and more impregnable basis the fabric of our liberties," he used the columns and leaders of his paper as a weapon of fearless and scathing criticism of those who attempted to defend

---

5  John Tyas' report was published in *The Times*, 19 August.

the action of the authorities on the 16th of August. As a single illustration we may mention that when, in May, 1821, Sir Francis Burdett[6] moved in the House of Commons for a Committee of inquiry into the whole question, and the motion was seconded by Mr. Hobhouse,[7] and lost by more than two to one, Taylor devoted nine and a half crowded columns to a report, and criticised the debate in a leader consisting of three columns closely printed in small type.

Taylor's vigorous and spirited protests brought out Mr. Francis Phillips, a Manchester manufacturer, as champion of the magistrates, and his able pamphlet entitled "An Exposure of the Calumnies Circulated by the Enemies of Social Order against the Magistrates and the Yeomanry Cavalry," went through two editions of a thousand each. The controversy was the signal for the appearance of a perfect avalanche of tracts, among which we must at least mention two: an anonymous paper entitled, "An Impartial Narrative of the Late Melancholy Occurrences in Manchester"; and a high-toned protest entitled, "A Letter from J.C. Hobhouse, F.R.S., to Lord Viscount Castlereagh".[8]

More interesting for our present purpose are the detailed narratives of a number of eye-witnesses of the scene in St. Peter's fields. The most famous of these is the account given by Samuel Bamford,[9] the Middleton weaver, in his *Passages in the Life of a Radical*.[10] Corroborative of Bamford's narrative is the story written by a man who occupied a very different station in life,

---

6  Burdett was a reformist politician who was very critical of the government. For instance, in 1820 he was fined £1000 and imprisoned for three months for "composing, writing, and publishing a seditious libel" in highlighting the cruelties at Peterloo.

7  John Hobhouse was a Radical politician. While a candidate for election, he wrote a pamphlet in favour of Reform which was deemed a breach of parliamentary privilege. His subsequent imprisonment increased his popularity and he was elected as MP for Westminster in 1820. Hobhouse was a great friend of the poet Lord Byron.

8  Viscount Castlereagh was the leader of the House of Commons.

9  A Radical Reformer and writer. He had been a weaver and warehouseman. Bamford was present at Peterloo and was imprisoned for a year for incitement to riot, despite there being no evidence that he or his group had been involved in violence.

10  Published in 1840 and details the life of the English working classes at the time of Peterloo.

John Benjamin Smith,[11] afterwards first treasurer of the Anti-Corn Law League,[12] and a close friend of John Bright.[13] A third connected narrative is given by Archibald Prentice,[14] in his *Recollections of Manchester*. There is also, of course, the rather highly coloured account given by Hunt,[15] the chairman of the meeting, in his *Memoirs*,[16] issued during his confinement in Ilchester jail.[17]

One of the most valuable of all the individual narratives is that given by the Rev. Edward Stanley, father of Dean Stanley, and brother of the first Baron Stanley of Alderley, who came upon the scene quite unintentionally and by pure accident, and watched the proceedings from beginning to end from the room immediately above that in which the magistrates were assembled. Stanley was at the time Rector of Alderley; he afterwards became Bishop of Norwich. His testimony—which was accompanied by a small sketch-plan[18]—is specially valuable because he was pre-eminently a statistician; he became, indeed, one of the first Presidents of the Manchester Statistical Society. Moreover, he saw everything from the point of view of a stranger from outside; and his effort to be impartial and to confine himself to measured language is almost laboured.

The events at Peterloo gave rise to no less than six trials in the various courts, at which the story of the day's proceedings was told and retold with the most wearisome reiteration. The chairman of the magistrates,

---

11 A Liberal MP who was a merchant, a justice of the peace and president of the Manchester Chamber of Commerce.

12 The Corn Laws imposed tariffs on imported wheat, which allowed farmers to charge more thereby increasing the cost of bread. The League sought to repeal the laws so as to help poorer people afford cheaper food.

13 A Quaker who was also a Radical and Liberal politician. Co-founder of the Anti-Corn Law League.

14 A Scottish journalist and Radical who helped found the Anti-Corn Law League.

15 Henry Hunt (1773–1835). Known as "Orator" for his rousing speeches in favour of Radical Reform. He was a wealthy farmer and was drawn to Radicalism shortly after the Napoleonic Wars.

16 *Memoirs of Henry Hunt, Esq.* in three volumes is subtitled "written by himself in His Majesty's Jail at Ilchester", published in 1820–2.

17 Ilchester County Gaol and House of Correction had opened in 1615 and closed in 1843. Ilchester is some 200 miles from Manchester. While in prison, as well as his *Memoirs*, Hunt also wrote *A Peep into a Prison; or, the Inside of Ilchester Bastile*, published in 1821, detailing the horrific conditions he found there.

18 See page 54.

the special constables, the yeomanry, the Reformers, the anti-Reformers, the chairman of the meeting, the reporters for the London and provincial papers—all were allowed to have their say, and once more the Rev. Edward Stanley appeared as a witness.

More than a quarter of a century after the event, Sir William Jolliffe, Bart., M.P., who actually rode as an officer in the charge of the 15th Hussars at Peterloo, wrote a detailed account of the day from the soldier's standpoint. This valuable record was inserted in *The Life of Lord Sidmouth*, for which it had been prepared. Lastly, complimentary dinners in Manchester gave to the commanders of the yeomanry engaged an opportunity of presenting their point of view which was duly reported.

We have now enumerated the principal sources upon which we have to depend for the details of this eventful day; before attempting a picture of the scene it is necessary to say something of the state of Manchester and of the country at the time.

# The Unrest that Followed the Napoleonic Wars

## *Frequent use of the military by the civil authorities*

THE EMPLOYMENT OF MOUNTED troops and infantry in quelling civil disturbances, protecting property, and dispersing crowds was a common practice for years before the catastrophe in St. Peter's fields; and, of course, troops were used subsequently, especially during the Chartist[19] disturbances just twenty years later, when Sir Charles Napier was placed in command of nearly 6000 men in the north, and stationed 2000 of them at Manchester, which he regarded as a danger centre. We must, however, carefully distinguish between cases where there was open riot, and instances where there was not even a threat of disorder. At the famous Shude Hill Fight in 1757,[20] the soldiers were only ordered to fire when one of their number had been killed and nine wounded by the rioters. The result of the volley was that four people were killed and fifteen wounded. In 1812 Shude Hill was again the scene of disorder, when the cavalry were called in and the Riot Act was read. In the same year the great depression led to disorder

---

19 A working-class movement from 1838 to 1857 that tried to get Parliament to accept the People's Charter that consisted of six reforms: (1) A vote for every man over 21 years of age, of sound mind, and not undergoing punishment for a crime. (2) The secret ballot to protect the elector in the exercise of his vote. (3) No property qualification for MPs in order to allow the constituencies to return the man of their choice. (4) Payment of MPs, enabling tradesmen, working men, or other persons of modest means to leave or interrupt their livelihood to attend to the interests of the nation. (5) Equal constituencies, securing the same amount of representation for the same number of electors, instead of allowing less populous constituencies to have as much or more weight than larger ones. (6) Annual parliamentary elections, thus presenting the most effectual check to bribery and intimidation, since no purse could buy a constituency under a system of universal manhood suffrage in each 12-month period. Chartism failed directly to reform Parliament but eventually all of its aims were brought about except for annual Parliaments.

20 Shudehill in Manchester, near to the present-day Arndale Centre, was the site of a food riot.

at Stockport, when a troop of the Cheshire yeomanry "cleared an area of a hundred acres in less than ten minutes". This year also saw very serious machine riots at Middleton,[21] where the Scots Greys and Cumberland Militia were used with fatal results.

At the conclusion of the Napoleonic war the Corn Bill led to fresh disturbances, which continued, more or less, up to the date of Peterloo, the chief causes being unemployment, the scarcity of food, and the terrible social and economic conditions under which the operatives and their families lived. We may form some faint conception of these conditions by reading such a Report as that issued by Dr. Kay (afterwards Sir James Kay Shuttleworth) years after the date of Peterloo.[22] The details he gives as to the sanitary conditions in Manchester are such that we could hardly quote them here. Between 1750 and 1820, it must be remembered, the population of Manchester increased sevenfold; yet the town was still under the old manorial system, with no local government whatever; and the great mass of its inhabitants—it is this that makes the situation so cruel— were, in a public sense, *inarticulate*, for Manchester had no parliamentary representative. "The overworked population," writes Dr. Kay, "had scarcely any means of education, except Sunday schools, dame schools, and adventure schools. They were ignorant, harassed with toil, inflamed with drink, and often goaded with want, owing to sudden depressions of trade." In a memorial sent up to Lord Sidmouth, the Home Secretary, only a few weeks before the catastrophe of Peterloo, the magistrates sitting at the New Bailey Courthouse in Salford make pointed reference to "the deep distresses of the manufacturing classes of this extensive population," and go so far as to say: "when the people are oppressed with hunger we do not wonder at their giving ear to any doctrines which they are told will redress their grievances."

In the years 1815 and 1816 the masses were already feeling their way towards a solution of their difficulties. The writings of Cobbett[23] were

---

21 Middleton is about 5 miles from Manchester and was the site of a "Luddite" riot where there was anger at the use of steam looms in a mill. The factory owner had armed his workers and at least five rioters were killed.

22 Dr. Kay was a medical doctor and wrote *The Moral and Physical Condition of the Working Class Employed in the Cotton Manufacture in Manchester*, published in 1832. He acquired "Shutttleworth" from his wife, who was a rich heiress.

23 William Cobbett was a reforming MP with strong views on ending corruption in politics.

eagerly read; Hampden clubs[24] were formed in the distressed districts; and Universal Suffrage, Annual Parliaments, and a Reform of the Currency were held up as the sovereign cure for the ills of the workers. Hence the agitators earned for themselves the name of "Reformers". In addition to Cobbett, the workers looked up to five or six public men as their leaders and champions, and one of these became the hero of the Peterloo massacre. They were, Sir Francis Burdett, Lord Cochrane, Major Cartwright, Sir Charles Wolseley, Mr. Henry Hunt, and—at one part of his career—Lord Brougham.

In attempting to understand the situation, it is advisable to keep two facts in mind: first, that there was, without doubt, secret plotting in a few isolated cases among the operatives, of a decidedly dangerous character; this is freely admitted by their own representative, who tells, e.g. of the scheme to make a "Moscow of Manchester";[25] secondly, that the discovery of this fact led to an estrangement between employers and employed, which postponed and delayed any approach to a friendly settlement.

The whole situation is well expressed by the anonymous author of *An Impartial Narrative*,[26] when he says: "The two general classes of Reformers and Anti-Reformers *watched each other with a jealous eye*". To anyone who makes an earnest attempt to obtain an impartial view, this attitude of mutual suspicion, which seemed to heighten the barrier between the two classes as time went on, is one of the most painful features of the whole story.

Two years before Peterloo, when the Habeas Corpus Act[27] had already been suspended, and a number of the agitators were consequently in hiding, a meeting was held in St. Peter's fields which, in all respects except the massacre, was almost the counterpart of the Peterloo meeting. On the 10th

---

24  Named after John Hampden who was a Parliamentarian soldier during the English Civil War. He died of his wounds in 1643. The clubs were formed as part of the Radical movement that was emerging at the time of Peterloo.

25  This refers to when the French army invaded Russia in 1812 and the Russians burned and abandoned Moscow before Napoleon seized it.

26  *An Impartial Narrative of the Late Melancholy Occurrences in Manchester,* published in 1819.

27  This Act suspended habeus corpus, which was the right to be brought before a court on being arrested. The home secretary, Lord Sidmouth, removed this right because he determined that "a traitorous conspiracy ... [existed] for the purpose of overthrowing ... the established government". And that there was "a malignant spirit which had brought such disgrace upon the domestic character of the people" and "had long prevailed in the country, but especially since the commencement of the French Revolution".

of March a great crowd assembled to give a send-off to the "Blanketeers".[28] The magistrates were alarmed at the prospect, though nothing was proposed but a march of a body of petitioners to London, and on the 8th of March the Lord Lieutenant authorised Sir John Leycester to call out the Cheshire Yeomanry in aid of the civil power. The order was obeyed with alacrity; on the following day five troops of that regiment assembled and marched for Manchester, where they joined the King's Dragoon Guards, and detachments of the 54th and 85th Infantry, the whole force being under the command of Sir John Byng.

Early on the morning of the 10th crowds of people began to stream into the town by various roads, many carrying knapsacks and blankets. The instigators of the meeting spoke from improvised hustings in St. Peter's fields. The magistrates met in the very same room which they afterwards occupied on the occasion of Peterloo, and having warned the leaders with no result, they called upon the military, as they afterwards did at Peterloo, to disperse the meeting. By a "judicious movement" of the King's Dragoon Guards, the cart was instantly surrounded and the constables took the whole of the speakers into custody. No opposition was offered to the cavalry, and the multitude immediately dispersed, the troops giving them free passage. The march of the Blanketeers was then harassed by the mounted troops mentioned above, all the way to Macclesfield, where a number of arrests were made, and this effort of the Reformers eventually fizzled out. The circumstances of the meeting should be compared with those of Peterloo, because—as Mr. J. E. Taylor afterwards pointed out: "Here is to be found the precedent for that novel form of reading the Riot Act (if in either case it were read at all) which was followed on the 16th of August, 1819". Immediately after the Blanket meeting, the Government set on foot a system of espionage, which greatly embittered those agitating for Reform, and was severely criticised in Parliament. Meanwhile the privileged classes in Manchester and other towns had already met, at the suggestion of the Home Secretary, to consider "the necessity of adopting additional measures for the maintenance of the public peace". Thus repressive measures only drove the discontent under to smoulder, and suspicion helped to widen the breach. The principal perpetrators of this policy, afterwards so pointedly anathematised by Shelley,[29] were Lord Sidmouth, the Home Secretary,

---

28 The Blanket March was a group of Lancashire weavers who planned to march the 200 miles to London to present petitions to the Price Regent to ask for improvements in the cotton trade.

29 Shelley's "Mask of Anarchy" appears at the end of this book (page 57).

Eldon the Lord Chancellor, and Viscount Castlereagh, the Secretary for foreign affairs.

Less than a year before Peterloo, in September, 1818, the Dragoons were once more called out to disperse a crowd of "turned-out" spinners who were attacking a mill in Ancoats. Evidently this was the scene which Mrs. Gaskell had in her mind when picturing the attack on Mr. Thornton's mill in *North and South*.[30] It must not be forgotten that there was, at the time under consideration, no regular police force available.[31] Nadin, the deputy constable, who figures in the various arrests, was merely the paid official of the antiquated Court Leet.[32] The so-called "Commission of Police," which was under the control of an absurdly unrepresentative committee, will not bear comparison with the Watch Committees of to-day. The practice of swearing-in special constables was frequently resorted to, but special constables had none of the skill and training in the matter of handling crowds possessed by modern police. The constables sometimes declined to act without military aid, and the magistrates leaned heavily on the support afforded by the troops in their difficulties, and frequently acknowledged their indebtedness to them. It is indeed evident from the history of the Cheshire Yeomanry, that when the question of disbanding that regiment was seriously discussed, as it was in the early part of the nineteenth century, it was overruled by the consideration that the troops were indispensable in dealing with civil disturbances, and the chairman of the sessions immediately following the meeting of Blanketeers in March, 1817, took occasion to say that "the districts most liable to disturbance derived effective military aid from a corps formed in a neighbouring and for the most part tranquil county"; and again, that *"the Bench would be most happy to further any proposition for forming such a corps in the manufacturing districts"*.

It must not be forgotten that the "neighbouring and for the most part tranquil county" was an agricultural district; and that the farmers and country squires who rode in its yeomanry had a special interest in preserving intact the Corn Law, which the Reformers were out to repeal.

---

30  Elizabeth Gaskell published this novel in 1854.

31  London was the first city to form a police service in 1829. By the 1850s, forces were established nationally.

32  A manorial court which belonged to feudal times. Bizarrely, some still exist today although their roles are now traditional or ceremonial.

# The Manchester and Salford Yeomanry

THE RESOLUTION JUST QUOTED is of great importance for a proper understanding of the occurrences at Peterloo. A careful examination of the evidence makes it clear that the catastrophe was (as far as can be seen now) largely due to the employment at the outset of a body of volunteer cavalry known as the "Manchester and Salford Yeomanry". It is not easy to trace the history of these troops; no contemporary records seem to exist. We can, however, fix the date of their formation within a few months. In his famous tract entitled "An Exposure of the Calumnies," etc., Mr. Francis Phillips, in quoting a letter of thanks from Lord Sidmouth to the commander of the Cheshire Yeomanry, dated the 12th of March, 1817, says (Appendix, p. v) "*The Manchester Yeomanry had not then been embodied*". Yet Aston, in his *Metrical Records of Manchester*, states that the Corps was formed in 1817, and gives some details of its inception. We are therefore justified in supposing that it was embodied as the result of the Resolution quoted above; in other words, that (apparently in emulation of the Cheshire Yeomanry) the corps was instituted mainly for the purpose of assisting the civil authorities in maintaining order. With reference to the number employed at Peterloo Mr. Phillips speaks (p. 58) of "the 116 Manchester and Salford Yeomen who were on duty on the 16th of August". The actual names, addresses, and occupations of these men are given in the *Manchester Observer* for the 20th of April, 1822, and this, again, is important evidence. They are nearly all from Manchester, a few coming from Pendleton and Stretford; mostly tradesmen, innkeepers, and small manufacturers, e.g. cheesemongers, ironmongers, tailors, watchmakers, calico-printers,[33] butchers, corn-merchants, butter factors, and so on. It would be unreasonable to suppose that such a levy would contain many skilled horsemen, and this, as we shall see, was fully borne out at Peterloo. Lieutenant Jolliffe says of them: "without the knowledge possessed by a (strictly speaking) military body, they were placed, most unwisely, as it appeared, under the immediate command of the civil authorities"; and this "greatly aggravated the disasters of the day".

It may easily be supposed that the use of these local levies of mounted troops for purposes of this kind aroused bitter resentment in the minds of the labouring population, which only grew as time went on. Thus we

---

33 This involved using wooden blocks and dyes to colour unbleached cotton fabric.

need not be surprised to find these words in the *Manchester Observer* just a month before the tragedy of Peterloo: "The stupid boobies of yeomanry cavalry in the neighbourhood have only just made the discovery that the mind and muscle of the country are at length united, and during the past week have been foaming and broiling themselves to death in getting their swords ground and their pistols examined. ... The yeomanry are, generally speaking, the fawning dependents of the great, with a few fools and a greater proportion of coxcombs, who imagine they acquire considerable importance by wearing regimentals."

The sharpening of the swords, by the way, was fully acknowledged by the other side. Thus Mr. Phillips writes (p. 17): "The simple history of all the tales we have heard of sharpening sabres is briefly this. On the 7th of July the Government issued orders to the Cheshire and Manchester Yeomanry Cavalry, through the Lords Lieutenant, to hold themselves in readiness, and consequently most of the Manchester Cavalry sent their arms to the same cutler which the corps during the last war had employed, to put them in condition". All these details are important as aggravating the bitter feelings which already existed, and we shall see later that when this improvised corps advanced into the crowd, using their sharpened swords, they were in some cases individually recognised by those at whom they struck. As we approach the date of Peterloo, the confidence reposed in the volunteer cavalry by the authorities becomes even more apparent, and about a month before the event the Commander of the Cheshire Yeomanry received orders to hold his regiment in readiness at a moment's notice to aid the civil power.

Meanwhile the magistrates complained to the Home Secretary that as the law stood they were "unable to interfere with the meetings of the Reformers, notwithstanding their decided conviction of their mischief and danger," and that "upon this most important point they were unarmed". These are the very words which Mr. L.C. Hobhouse took as his text in the able letter to Lord Castlereagh mentioned above.

# The Drillings

WE COME, LASTLY, TO another phase of the agitation, which was strongly developed not long before Peterloo, and—being undoubtedly misunderstood—gave the authorities some anxiety: the Reformers began to hold meetings on the moors and elsewhere for drill[34] in squads. Bamford has left a very graphic account of these "drilling parties," as he calls them. He emphasises the fact that there were "no armed meetings," "no concealed meetings," or "anything of the sort". His explanation of the object of the drills—and there seems to be no reason why the explanation should not be accepted—is as follows: "It was deemed expedient that the meeting on the 16th of August should be as morally effective as possible, and that it should exhibit a spectacle such as had never before been witnessed in England. We had frequently been taunted in the public press with our ragged, dirty appearance at these assemblages; with the confusion of our proceedings, and the moblike crowds in which our numbers were mustered; and we determined that for once, at least, these reflections should not be deserved—that we would disarm the bitterness of our political opponents by a display of cleanliness, sobriety, and decorum such as we never before had exhibited. ... We obtained by these drilling parties all we sought or thought of—an expertness and order while moving in bodies."

It is certainly true that this was the effect of the drilling; the order with which the various contingents approached the rendezvous on the fateful day was commended alike by friend and foe; in fact one of the magistrates afterwards stated on oath that it was not until he saw "the party come on the field in beautiful order that he became alarmed". It is easy for those of us who know the beautiful green uplands to which Bamford refers, to believe his statement that "to the sedentary weavers and spinners these drillings on the open moors were periods of healthful exercise and enjoyment". His description of them is one of the most charming passages in all his writings; and surely it is a happy coincidence that the centenary of Peterloo should see the Tandle Hills—the very hills he describes—thrown open to the public for ever.[35]

---

34  That is military-style training.

35  In 1919, the owner gave the park to the people of Royton as an "offering for peace after the Great European War 1914–1919". (The year 1919, rather than 1918, is used on some memorials as this was the year in which the peace treaty ending the conflict was signed.)

The authorities saw fit to take quite another view of the drills. On the very day before the event of Peterloo a large meeting for such exercises was held on White Moss, near Middleton, very early in the morning, and a few men who were there for purposes of espionage, and who afterwards reported to the magistrates, were very roughly handled by the operatives. Bamford does not hesitate to say that the rough treatment accorded to these spies "probably eradicated from the minds of the magistrates and our opponents whatever sentiments of indulgence they may hitherto have retained towards us". This was on the day preceding Peterloo; on the day following the event the magistrates met and denounced the meetings for drill as "contrary to law".

# The Story of Peterloo

THE GREAT MEETING PLANNED to be held in St. Peter's fields on the
9th of August, 1819, seems to have originated in a desire on the part
of the Reformers of the Manchester district to emulate the example set by
other towns in the country, notably that of London and Birmingham, where
great gatherings brought together to advocate Reform had been addressed
by Mr. Henry Hunt, and other leaders in the movement for the better representation of the working classes. The advertisement which appeared in the
*Manchester Observer* for the 31st of July, 1819, ran: "The Public are respect-
fully informed that a meeting will be held here on Monday, the 9th of
August, 1819, on the area near St. Peter's Church, to take into consideration
the most speedy and effectual mode of obtaining Radical Reform in the
Commons House of Parliament, being fully convinced that nothing less
can remove the intolerable evils under which the People of this Country
have so long, and do still, groan; and also to consider the propriety of the
Unrepresented Inhabitants of Manchester electing a Person to represent
them in Parliament, and the adopting Major Cartwright's Bill. H. Hunt in
the chair."

On the very next day the *Manchester Chronicle*, a superior Tory organ,
published a letter from Lord Sidmouth to the Lord Lieutenant of Cheshire
emphasising the need for the utmost vigilance on the part of the magistrates on account of the frequent public meetings, and desiring him to give
immediate directions to the several Corps of Yeomanry Cavalry to hold
themselves in readiness to attend to any call for support and assistance they
may receive from the bench.

A week later the magistrates proclaimed the proposed meeting to be
illegal. The Reformers accordingly decided to take the advice of counsel,
and Mr. Saxton, sub-editor of the *Observer*, was commissioned to proceed to Liverpool and seek legal advice in the matter. He returned with
the important ruling, "that the intention of choosing Representatives,
contrary to the existing law, tends greatly to render the proposed meeting
seditious". Accepting this ruling, the Reformers at once abandoned the
meeting and carefully revised their programme. Accordingly, on the 7th of
August, the *Observer* published a notice to the effect that the Boroughreeve
and Constables (i.e. the three main officials of the Court Leet) had been
requested by 700 persons to summon a meeting "to consider the propriety
of adopting the most *legal* and *effectual* means of obtaining Reform in the
Commons House of Parliament," and had declined to do so. Notice was
therefore given (over the signatures of nearly 1300 inhabitants) that a meet-

ing would be held in St. Peter's fields on Monday, the 16th of August, and that Mr. Henry Hunt would take the chair at 12 o'clock.

A week later, on the 14th of August, the *Observer* contained a long letter from Henry Hunt, dated from Smedley Cottage, where he was the guest of Mr. Johnson, urging the importance of the Reformers exhibiting "a steady, firm, and temperate deportment," and bringing with them "no other weapon than that of an approving conscience". According to the *Chronicle* there was an influx of strangers on the Saturday and Sunday preceding the eventful Monday. The same paper speaks of "painful anticipation" on the Sunday as to "how the following day would terminate". The general opinion on 'Change[36] on the Saturday was that the magistrates had decided not to disturb the meeting, unless some breach of the peace occurred, and men of all parties said that the meeting would go off quietly. No disturbance of any kind took place in Manchester on Sunday, the 15th of August.

It was a grand opportunity for a man with *vision*; but the responsible authorities—i.e. the special Committee of the magistrates of Lancashire and Cheshire (which included three clergymen) meeting in Manchester—seem to have been in a panic. They sat till midnight on Sunday without being able to decide what to do. At 11 p.m. one of them wrote to the Home Secretary that although the magistrates, as then advised, did not then think of preventing the meeting, they were alarmed, and were in a state of painful uncertainty.

The long-expected day came at last. The morning was fine, and later on the heat was considerable. In Manchester the magistrates saw fit to publish a notice recommending the peaceable and well-disposed inhabitants to remain in their own houses during the whole day, and to keep their children and servants within doors. The Rev. Jeremiah Smith, then the High Master of the Free Grammar School, afterwards stated at the Trial that most of the shop windows were closed, and that as there was a general feeling of apprehension, he dismissed his day boys after breakfast, and eventually went home and locked himself and his boarders into his house in Long Millgate—the very house from which the boy De Quincey[37] had slipped

---

36 The Manchester Exchange was a place for business transactions, such as the sale of stocks and shares. It had been the site of a riot in 1812.

37 Thomas De Quincey (1785–1859) was a journalist and essayist best known for documenting his opioid addiction in the 1821 book *Confessions of an English Opium-Eater.*

away "in the deep lustre of a cloudless July morning,"[38] not twenty years before.

As early as nine in the morning people began to assemble in St. Peter's fields. The magistrates met first at the Star Inn and at eleven o'clock adjourned to the house of Mr. Buxton in Mount Street. By this time the troops employed had been posted out of sight in the streets lying just off the open space where the gathering was held. Their disposition seems to have been as follows: one troop of the Manchester and Salford Yeomanry was concealed in Pickford's yard, off Portland Street, another troop seems to have been in Byrom Street; their commander was Major Trafford, but the first troop seems to have been led on this occasion by Hugh Birley, who only a few years before had opposed the new Corn Law. The Cheshire Yeomanry, in their full strength of eight troops, i.e. at least 400 men, had assembled on Sale moor at 9 a.m. and arrived at their assigned station in St. John Street soon after eleven; two squadrons of the 15th Hussars (i.e. over 300 men) were in Byrom Street and a troop of the same regiment was in Lower Mosley Street, acting as escort to a troop of the Royal Horse Artillery with two long six-pounders; the guns thus commanded the principal approach to the area. The above are the mounted troops; besides these nearly the whole of the 31st Infantry were concealed in Brasenose Street; and several companies of the 88th Infantry were "in ambush" in the neighbourhood of Dickinson Street; the names of the commanders of all these detachments are given, and the whole force was under the direction of Lieut.-Colonel L'Estrange.

The hustings, which consisted of two carts and some boards, were erected just below Windmill Street, about 100 yards from Mount Street. The speakers faced northwards, towards the Friends' Meeting House, close to which was the Friends' school. Here, near a few oak trees, a quantity of loose timber was lying about, of which we shall hear later on. It was about 12 o'clock when a strong double cordon of several hundred special constables was drawn between Mr. Buxton's house in Mount Street and the hustings. They formed a lane by which, if necessary, the magistrates could communicate with the speakers.

---

38 The quotation should be "with the radiant lustre of a cloudless July morning".

# The Processions from the Outlying Districts

WE MUST NOW TURN to the districts outside Manchester, where preparations were early afoot for the great meeting. Detachments of Reformers were streaming along the main roads towards Manchester, with bands playing and banners flying, and caps of liberty held aloft. These were red peaked caps, of Phrygian shape, and had been used as symbols by the Revolutionists in France. The cap is supposed to have been employed as a symbol of the manumission of a slave in Roman times.[39]

We have actual details of several of these processions—the Middleton, Royton, and Chadderton parties, the Rochdale section, the Saddleworth troop, the Oldham group, and those from Stockport, from Pendleton, from Ashton, and from Bury. The march of the Middleton and Rochdale detachments is graphically described by Bamford, who led the first, the whole contingent numbering, according to his estimate, about 6000 men, with numbers of women and children.

By 8 a.m. all Middleton was astir. The procession was arranged with a band of youths in front wearing laurels, then came representatives of the various districts, five abreast, then the band and the colours. These bore the inscriptions: "Unity and Strength"; "Liberty and Fraternity";[40] "Parliaments Annual"; "Suffrage Universal". A crimson velvet cap inscribed "Libertas" was carried among the banners. Then came, five abreast, the delegates from eighteen different districts. At the sound of a bugle, some 3000 formed a hollow square and Bamford addressed them, enjoining them to be steadfast and serious, not to offer resistance if their leaders were arrested, and to lay aside their sticks. This last injunction Bamford communicated to them, in accordance with general orders, somewhat against his will. He speaks of his contingent as "a most respectable assemblage of labouring men, all decently, though humbly, attired". "My address," he adds, "was received with cheers; it was heartily and unanimously assented to; we opened into

---

39 These caps made in a soft fabric were known as *bonnets rouge* during the French Revolution. There was on and off suppression of wearing the *bonnets* but they did reappear during Napoleon's 'Hundred Days'. This period included the Battle of Waterloo (15 June to 8 July 1815), which was four years prior to the events of Peterloo.

40 Similar to the French revolutionary *Liberté, égalité, fraternité*: liberty, equaliy, fraternity. The protesters perhaps felt 'equality' a little too much of a demand.

column—the music struck up—the banners flashed in the sunlight—other music was heard—it was that of the Rochdale party, coming to join us—we met—and a shout from 10,000 startled the echoes of the woods and dingles. Then all was quiet save the breath of music; and with intent seriousness we went on". The party included some hundreds of married women and several hundred girls, who danced and sang. "And thus, accompanied by our friends, and our dearest and most tender associations, we went slowly towards Manchester". We may stand by Bamford's monument in Middleton churchyard to-day, and looking down the hill, picture the scene. On the monument are inscribed these words of John Bright: "Bamford was a Reformer when to be so was unsafe, and he suffered for his faith".

Leaving these, we turn to the Oldham contingent. They met on the village green, Bent Grange, at nine, and were there joined by the Chadderton section. The Chadderton banner is still in existence. It was made of white and green silk, measured about 12 feet by 9 feet, and bore the usual mottoes of the Reformers. The Royton section carried two banners of red and green silk. The second is of special interest; it was inscribed "The Royton Female Union—Let us DIE like Men and Not be Sold like Slaves".[41] It was afterwards captured by the Cheshire Yeomanry and was produced as "evidence" against the Reformers in the Trial at York in the following year. The most beautiful of all the banners was said to be one of white silk carried by the Oldham people. But the banner which furnished the most important "evidence" in the Trial at York was a black one carried in the procession of the Saddleworth, Lees, and Mossley Union. It was inscribed: "Equal Representation or Death," "Unite and be Free," "No Boroughmongering,"[42] "Taxation without Representation is Unjust and Tyrannical," and it bore figures of Justice holding the scales and two hands clasped. After the lapse of a century the talk of the terrible danger hidden behind this banner, on the part of counsel at the Trial and public speakers elsewhere, may appear somewhat ludicrous. The Oldham and Royton colours were escorted by some 200 women dressed in white. The procession was joined later by the

---

41 The line "Let's die like men, and not be sold like slaves" appears in a play from 1682 called *Venice Preserved* by Thomas Otway. The play's themes feature political intrigue, corrupt politics and women's suffering. In the parliamentary debates that followed the Peterloo massacre it was recorded that: "Could any one doubt that such inscriptions, sanctioned as they must have been, by the immense assemblage before whom they were carried, were calculated to strike terror into all peaceable subjects?"

42 This is the sale of parliamentary seats.

Failsworth Radicals. Altogether there seem to have been sixteen banners displayed at the meeting, with five caps of liberty.

As the contingents approached Manchester, horsemen rode out in various directions to meet them and returned to report to the assembled magistrates. One of these scouts was Mr. Francis Phillips. In his "Exposure" he tells how he rode "along the turnpike road[43] leading to Stockport, and at a place called Ardwick Green, about one and a half miles from Manchester Exchange" met a regiment of Reformers marching in file, principally three deep. This column, 1400 or 1500 strong, "marched extremely well, observing the step though without music". It included about forty women, and the colours were handsome and inscribed "No Corn Laws" and "Universal Suffrage". Mr. Phillips is careful to add: "Nearly half of the men carried stout sticks". He slipped back to Manchester by another road and reported these facts to the magistrates. Immediately afterwards the column carried its colours into St. Peter's fields, and Phillips then took up his station in the cordon of special constables. From the evidence at the Trials we obtain details of the Bury contingent, five abreast and 3000 strong, with many women, and of that from Pendleton; and the Rev. Edward Stanley tells how he met the Reformers from Ashton.

Mr. Archibald Prentice, standing at a window, watched the crowd stream down Mosley Street. "I never," he says, "saw a gayer spectacle. There were haggard-looking men, certainly, but the majority were young persons, in their best Sunday suits, and the light-coloured dresses of the cheerful, tidy-looking women relieved the effect of the dark fustians[44] worn by the men. The 'marching order' of which so much was said afterwards, was what we often see now in the processions of Sunday School children and Temperance Societies. To our eyes the numerous flags seemed to have been brought to add to the picturesque effect of the pageant. Slowly and orderly the multitude took their places round the hustings. Our party laughed at the fears of the magistrates, and the remark was that if the men intended mischief they would not have brought their wives or their children with them. I passed round the outskirts of the meeting and mingled with the groups that stood chattering there. I occasionally asked the women if they were not afraid to be there, and the usual laughing reply was: 'What have we to be afraid of?' "

---

43 A toll road.

44 A type of coarse fabric made from cotton chiefly worn by labourers. Radicals chose to wear this fabric to show their allegiance to the Reform movement.

Mr. John Benjamin Smith, who watched the meeting from a window in Mrs. Orton's house, next door to Mr. Buxton's in Mount Street, says: "We reached there about eleven-thirty, and on our way saw large bodies of men and women with bands playing, flags and banners bearing devices. There were crowds of people in all directions, full of humour, laughing and shouting and making fun. It seemed to be a gala day with the country people, who were mostly dressed in their best, and brought with them their wives, and when I saw boys and girls taking their father's hands in the procession, I observed to my aunt: 'These are the guarantee of their peaceful intentions, we need have no fears,' and so we passed on to Mrs. Orton's house."

For two hours the Yeomanry and Hussars remained at their stations dismounted. Occasionally a few of the officers would ride up to Deansgate to watch the procession. One of them writes: "During the greater portion of that period a solid mass of people moved along the street. They marched at a brisk pace, with ranks well closed up, five or six bands of music being interspersed. Mr. Hunt was in an open carriage, adorned with flags and drawn by the people. As soon as the great bulk of the procession had passed, we were ordered to stand to our horses."

Manchester at that time was the mere nucleus of the Manchester of to-day. Districts which now lie well within its boundaries were then outlying villages. Even in the heart of the city several of the main thoroughfares familiar to us did not then exist. Market Street was still a mere winding lane, in places only five yards broad from building to building; the Bill for widening and straightening this thoroughfare was passed just two years after Peterloo. The present Corporation Street and Victoria Street did not exist, and Deansgate had not been widened. The pavements in places were only 18 inches wide, and several accidents occurred on the day of Peterloo from falls into the cellars which were then used as living rooms. Bearing in mind these facts, it is easy to follow the various contingents as they converged towards St. Peter's fields, the principal procession being that of the chairman.

Henry Hunt was a country gentleman of Wiltshire, whose personal characteristics made him specially successful as a demagogue, and there is no doubt that he was perfectly sincere. Bamford, whose admiration for him waned in later years, describes him as "gentlemanly in his manner and attire, six feet and better in height, and extremely well formed". The white hat which he wore became the symbol of Radicalism. He was shrewd, quick at repartee, and had the copious flow of highly-coloured language which delights a crowd. He was exceptionally clever in handling a great gathering, and was always scrupulously careful to keep within the strict letter of the law. His vanity we can forgive, for he rendered yeoman service to

"ORATOR" HUNT, 1773–1835. CHAIRMAN OF THE PETERLOO MEETING.

the cause of Liberty, but his private life, the details of which are told with almost brutal candour by himself in his *Memoirs*, will not bear inspection. Of his political record he has no reason to be ashamed. He presented the earliest petition to Parliament for Women's Suffrage; he fought the battle of Reform in its darkest days; and he attacked the first Reform Bill, demanding the Ballot, Universal Suffrage, and the repeal of the Corn Laws. He has been compared in some respects to Wilkes.[45] "As a practical Reformer he failed because he never understood the place of compromise in politics, but he was a shrewd and far-seeing ideologue and a splendid political gladiator." Whatever may be the correct estimate of him there is no doubt that at the time we are considering he was the object of boundless admiration on the part of the Reformers, who simply idolised him. After he was bailed at Lancaster, pending his trial, he was accorded a triumphal procession through Lancashire to Manchester, and in London he was cheered to the echo by enormous crowds.

The contingents from Middleton and Rochdale, led by Samuel Bamford, were approaching Collyhurst, when a message reached them from Hunt, directing them to come by way of Newton and head his procession from Smedley Cottage. This they did, but taking a wrong turn at the top of Shude Hill, they led down Swan Street, Oldham Street, and Mosley Street, and swept round the left-hand corner, i.e. the south side of St. Peter's church into "a wide unbuilt space, occupied by an immense multitude, which opened and received them with loud cheers". Hunt's procession, meanwhile, took the route down Shude Hill, and—Corporation Street not being in existence—wound round Hanging Ditch, Old Millgate, the Market Place, and St. Mary's Gate into Deansgate, whence it emerged along the fragment of Peter Street and made for the hustings.

On the box-seat of the carriage in which Hunt rode sat Mrs. Mary Fildes, carrying a white silk flag as the president of the "Manchester Female Reformers". Mrs. Banks, in a note in the Appendix to her *Manchester Man*, states that this Mrs. Fildes was personally known to her. In her story she represents her as sabred at the hustings. We have already referred to the Female Reformers of Royton, and their banner of red and green silk. The Female Reformers of Manchester also had their banner and had planned to present it to Mr. Hunt after the meeting, with an address stating that "as wives, mothers, daughters, in their social, domestic, moral capacities, they came forward in the sacred cause of liberty, a cause in which their husbands, their fathers, and their sons had embarked the last hope of a suffering

45 John Wilkes (1725–97) was an MP and journalist and an early Reformer.

humanity". Still more interesting is the pathetic appeal which these Female Reformers of Manchester, who were well organised, issued before the meeting to "the Wives, Mothers, Sisters, and Daughters of the higher and middle classes of Society," describing the terrible privations which had made the petitioners "sick of life, and weary of a world where poverty, wretchedness, tyranny, and injustice had so long been allowed to reign among men"; and imploring these more favoured ladies to come forward and join hands with them in the struggle for Reform. The Committee of the Manchester Female Reformers, dressed in white, walked behind Hunt's carriage. They afterwards sent messages of sympathy to him, during his imprisonment in Ilminster jail. "Our tyrants," they said, "have immured you in a dungeon; but we have enshrined you in our hearts". On the expiration of his term, they presented to him a silver urn, suitably inscribed.

The woman on the box-seat was afterwards confused by the magistrates, in their Report to the Home Secretary, with a Mrs. Elizabeth Gaunt, who was found in the carriage, after the meeting, in a fainting condition. Taylor was quick to seize upon this instance of what he ironically termed "official accuracy". This poor woman had been wounded by the cavalry. She was nevertheless arrested, and confined for over a week at the New Bailey, when "the Court had great pleasure in ordering her immediate discharge".

As the carriage made its way across the square—Mr. Hunt standing up—a great shout arose from a crowd whose numbers have been variously estimated (Mr. Hunt told a London audience afterwards that there were 150,000!), but we shall probably not be far wrong if we put the figure at 60,000. Well might Bamford describe the scene as "solemnly impressive". Arrived at the hustings Hunt was at once voted to the chair, and taking off his white hat, he began his address.

We have abundant material to enable us to reconstruct the scene. Along part of the upper side of Windmill Street ran a row of houses. In front of these, on the slightly rising ground, stood a number of spectators, and the dense crowd reached from Windmill Street back towards the Friends' Meeting House on the north. Mount Street was bounded then on the east by a row of houses reaching, perhaps, one-third of the way along the present Midland hotel; the crowd did not reach right up to these houses, and there were stragglers in the intervening space. It was in this intervening space that the Manchester Yeomanry reined up later on as they arrived. Above the heads of the crowd, at intervals, could be seen the various banners and caps of liberty. Mr. Hunt and the other speakers were standing on the simple hustings facing northwards. The magistrates were watching the proceedings from a window on the first floor of the house of Mr. Buxton in Mount Street. At the window of the room immediately above them stood

THE HUNT MEMORIAL IN THE VESTIBULE OF THE
MANCHESTER REFORM CLUB.

the Rev. Edward Stanley, Rector of Alderley, an unintentional but keenly observant spectator of every detail. At one of the windows of the adjoining house stood Mr. J.B. Smith. All around, in the side streets, but not visible from St. Peter's fields, were posted the regular troops and the yeomanry, and mounted messengers for communication with them were in attendance at the magistrates' house. Among the representatives of the Press were Mr. John Tyas, for the London *Times*, Mr. Edward Baines for the *Leeds Mercury*, and Mr. John Smith for the *Liverpool Mercury*. Purely as a guess, we should be inclined to conjecture that the last of the three may have been the author of the anonymous *Impartial Narrative*.

The magistrates had at length come to a decision of some kind. If a few of the inhabitants of the town would put their names to a statement to the effect that they considered that the town was endangered by the meeting, that would justify them in arresting the leaders. Accordingly, Richard Owen and some thirty others, including Mr. Phillips, signed the necessary affidavit, and a warrant in accordance with it was drawn up, stating that "Richard Owen had made oath that Henry Hunt and others had arrived in a car at the area near St. Peter's church, that an immense mob had assembled, and that he considered the town in danger". Referring to this strange mode of procedure afterwards Sir Francis Burdett said: "If arrests are to follow opinions which may find a place in other men's heads, there is an end to Liberty". However weak their action may appear to us to-day, it was on this ground that Nadin, the deputy constable, was instructed by the magistrates to go and interrupt a great peaceful meeting by arresting the leaders. Nadin assured them that even with the hundreds of special constables at his disposal he could not carry out the arrests without the assistance of the military. Hunt had only been speaking for a minute or two, therefore, when riders were dispatched for the troops. It is difficult to understand why a single message was not sent to Lieut.-Colonel L'Estrange, who was in command of the whole force. By a strange fatality the magistrates, at the same instant that they sent for Colonel L'Estrange, despatched a horseman to Pickford's yard for the troop of Manchester Yeomanry concealed there, which they had chosen to retain under their own control. The message, which was produced at the Trial, was as follows: "To the Commanding Officer, Portland Street: Sir: As Chairman of the Select Committee of Magistrates, I request you to proceed immediately to Number 6, Mount Street, where the Magistrates are assembled. They conceive the civil power wholly inadequate to preserve the peace. I have the honour, etc., William Hulton." At the moment that this letter was sent, Mr. Hunt was, in an orderly manner, addressing a perfectly peaceful meeting of some 60,000 men, women, and children.

Judging from what followed, Colonel L'Estrange seems to have made a skilful disposition of the forces at his disposal, closing in the infantry on the square from several points, while he himself led the Hussars and the Cheshire Yeomanry by a rather circuitous route, viz., along Deansgate as far as Fleet Street (a street which then ran parallel to Great Bridgwater Street, on the site of the present Central Station), then along Fleet Street, and so up Lower Mosley Street, where the artillery were posted, to Windmill Street.

Meanwhile the troop of Manchester Yeomanry stationed in Pickford's yard had lost no time in obeying their summons, and not having so far to go, they were easily first on the spot. They came along Nicholas Street and down Cooper Street. As they advanced along this street "at a tolerably brisk pace," a woman, carrying her two-year-old child in her arms, watched them pass, and then attempted to cross the street. Just at the moment, one of the Yeomanry who had been kept behind, came past "at a hand-gallop". The woman was knocked down and stunned; the child was thrown several yards, fell on its head, and was killed. This was the first casualty. The sworn affidavits to this incident may be read in the "Hunt Memorial" papers at the Manchester Reform Club. We shall see in a moment that a woman was involved in the second casualty also.

The whole fortune of the day turned on what happened in the few minutes that followed. It must be remembered that the troop of Manchester Yeomanry that arrived on the scene first was a local levy formed not long before, for the purpose of aiding the civil power, and consisted largely of local tradesmen, who seem to have been stung by the taunts levelled at them by the labouring classes, whom they were intended to intimidate. There is no doubt that their horses were not under control and that they were therefore not qualified for the difficult task before them. A mere handful of trained mounted troops properly directed, can, by feints, by backing, by rearing, and by skilful manoeuvres, break up and move a large crowd without injury to anyone. All parties are agreed that the Yeomanry halted in disorder. Even Hunt noticed that and remarked upon it, though he was a hundred yards away. On this point we have the clear testimony of the chairman of the magistrates, Mr. Hulton, who in his evidence at the Trial said that "their horses being raw, and unused to the field, they appeared to him to be in a certain degree of confusion". Mr. Stanley, again, says: "They halted in great disorder, and so continued for the few minutes they remained. This disorder was attributed by several persons in the room to the undisciplined state of their horses, little accustomed to act together, and probably frightened by the shout of the populace which greeted their arrival." It is impossible to avoid asking whether the whole story might not have been a different one, if these undisciplined irregular troops had been held back, and the 15th Hussars—men who were wearing their Waterloo medals, won only four years before—had been employed instead. For be it remembered that up to this moment the magistrates had no intention of using troops to disperse the meeting—that was emphatically stated by Mr. Hulton at the Trial—their decision was to arrest the leaders, and they seem to have anticipated that when that was done, the meeting would disperse of itself, as had happened under exactly similar circumstances at the meeting of Blanketeers.

# The Charge of the Manchester Yeomanry

As it was, the Yeomanry wheeled and, accompanied by the deputy constable, rode through the crowd towards the hustings. Stanley marks them on his plan as starting from a point apparently not far from the entrance to the present Association Hall in Mount Street and riding (as his arrows show) straight for the platform.[46] As they did so they left something behind them on the ground. It was the body of a woman. Stanley marks the exact spot where this body lay, apparently lifeless, through the subsequent proceedings, after which it was carried into the house. This was the second casualty. The Yeomanry entered the crowd to the right of the cordon of special constables, but one of the special constables was killed also.

Stanley's account is as follows: "Hunt began his address. I could distinctly hear his voice. He had not spoken above a minute or two before the cavalry were sent for—the messengers, we were told, might be seen from a back window. I ran to that window from which I could see the road leading to a timber yard (I believe) at no great distance, where, as I entered the town, I had observed the Manchester Yeomanry stationed. I saw three horsemen riding off, one towards the timber yard, the others in the direction which I knew led to the cantonments of other cavalry. I immediately returned to the front window, anxiously awaiting the result. A slight commotion amongst a body of spectators, chiefly women, who occupied a mound of raised broken ground on the left and to the rear of the orators [the reference is to Windmill Street; Stanley admitted at the Trial that he had not heard the name], convinced me that they saw something which excited their fears. Many jumped down and they soon dispersed more rapidly. By this time the alarm was quickly spreading and I heard several voices exclaiming: 'The soldiers! the soldiers!'"

It is possible that this alarm may have been due to a skilful movement of the infantry in Dickinson Street on the other side of the square, which seems to have taken place at this moment. A witness at the Oldham inquest speaks of "a movement of the people near Windmill Hill. I saw the 88th formed into line, and supposed the movement on the Windmill occasioned by the junction of the 88th. The regiment formed into a sort of crescent, which prevented me from moving either way. I could not get away by any

---

46  Stanley's sketch map appears on page 54.

exertion. The regiment prevented persons getting either way". This is an excellent illustration of the manner in which troops skilfully handled can be used to baffle and break up a crowd.

We return to Stanley's narrative: "Another moment brought the cavalry into the field on a gallop, which they continued till the word was given for halting them. They halted in great disorder, and so continued for the few minutes they remained. Hunt had evidently seen their approach, his hand had been pointed towards them and it was clear from his gestures that he was addressing the mob respecting them."

As a matter of fact Hunt's words, which Stanley could not hear, were: "Stand firm my friends! you see they are in disorder already. This is a trick. Give them three cheers." Bamford also shouted: "Stand fast! they are riding upon us: Stand fast!" We are reminded involuntarily of Shelley's lines, written so far away yet with such striking intuition:—

> Let the horsemen's scimitars
> Wheel and flash, like sphereless stars
> Thirsting to eclipse their burning
> In a sea of death and mourning.
>
> Stand ye calm and resolute,
> Like a forest close and mute,
> With folded arms and looks which are
> Weapons of unvanquished war.

Stanley continues: "Hunt's words, whatever they were, excited a shout from those immediately about him which was re-echoed with fearful animation by the rest of the multitude. Ere that had subsided, the cavalry, the loyal spectators, and the special constables cheered loudly in return, and a pause ensued of about a minute or two. An officer and some few others then advanced rather in front of the troop, formed, as I before said, in much disorder, and with scarcely the semblance of a line, their sabres glistened in the air, and on they went direct for the hustings. At first, and for a few paces, their movement was not rapid, and there was some show of an attempt to follow their officer in regular succession, five or six abreast; but as Mr. Francis Phillips in his pamphlet observes, they soon 'increased their speed,' and with a zeal and ardour which might naturally be expected from men acting with delegated power against a foe by whom it is understood they had long been insulted with taunts of cowardice, continued their course, seeming individually to vie with each other which should be first.

"As the cavalry approached the dense mass of people they used their utmost efforts to escape, but so closely were they pressed in opposite direc-

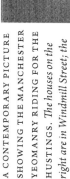

A CONTEMPORARY PICTURE SHOWING THE MANCHESTER YEOMANRY RIDING FOR THE HUSTINGS. *The houses on the right are in Windmill Street; the row on the left is in Mount Street. The hustings and the crowd to the right of the picture are on the site of the Free Trade Hall. The corner of the garden wall on the extreme left is on the site of the corner of the Midland Hotel. On the hustings we may distinguish Hunt and the President of the Manchester Female Reformers.*

tions by the soldiers, the special constables, the position of the hustings, and their own immense numbers that immediate escape was impossible. The rapid course of the troop was, of course, impeded when it came in contact with the mob, but a passage was forced in less than a minute—so rapid, indeed, was it that the guard of constables close to the hustings shared the fate of the rest. On their arrival at the hustings a scene of dreadful confusion ensued. The orators fell, or were forced off the scaffold in quick succession; fortunately for them, the stage being rather elevated, they were in great degree beyond the reach of the many swords which gleamed around them." In a footnote Stanley adds: "from the moment they began to force their way through the crowd towards the hustings, swords were up and swords were down, but whether they fell with the sharp or flat side I cannot, of course, pretend to give an opinion". Lieutenant Jolliffe decides this point for us when he says: "The Hussars drove the people forward with the flats of their swords; but sometimes, as is almost inevitably the case when men are placed in such situations, the edge was used, both by the Hussars and by the Yeomanry".

What actually happened at the hustings we know from the account given in the London *Times* by Tyas, who was present, and was himself taken into custody. "The officer who commanded the detachment," says *The Times*, "went up to Mr. Hunt and said, brandishing his sword: 'Sir, I have a warrant against you, and arrest you as my prisoner'. Mr. Hunt, after exhorting the people to tranquillity in a few words, turned round to the officer and said: 'I willingly surrender myself to any civil officer who will show me his warrant'. Nadin, the police officer, then came forward and said: 'I will arrest you: I have got information upon oath against you'. The same formality was gone through with Mr. Johnson. Mr. Hunt and Mr. Johnson then leaped from the waggon and surrendered themselves to the civil power." Stanley, who was a hundred yards away, says: "Hunt fell, or threw himself, amongst the constables, and was driven or dragged as fast as possible down the avenue which communicated with the magistrates' house; his associates were hurried after him in a similar manner. By this time so much dust had arisen that no accurate account can be given of what further took place at that particular spot. The square was now covered with the flying multitude, though still in parts the banners and caps of liberty were surrounded by groups."

All this was the work of a few minutes, and meanwhile the other troops had had time to arrive. Before we follow these into the crowd, it is right that we should listen to three other accounts of the charge of the Yeomanry. "The cavalry were in confusion," says Bamford, "they evidently could not, with all the weight of man and horse, penetrate that compact mass of human beings; and their sabres were plied to hew a way through naked held-up hands, and defenceless heads; and then chopped limbs, and wound-gaping skulls were seen; and groans and cries were mingled with the din of that horrid confusion. 'Ah! ah! for shame! for shame!' was shouted. Then 'Break! break! they are killing them in front, and they cannot get away'; and there was a general cry of 'Break! break!' For a moment the crowd held back as in a pause; then there was a rush, heavy and resistless as a headlong sea, and a sound like low thunder, with screams, prayers, and imprecations from the crowd-moiled,[47] and sabre-doomed, who could not escape." Bamford here does not distinguish between the charge of the Manchester Yeomanry and the charge of the Hussars, which followed a few minutes later. It was the latter that caused the "rush" of which he speaks. Though he was a man of five foot ten, and "stood on tiptoe" (as he tells us), he could not, being in the crowd, see everything. Stanley says emphatically: "No spectator on the ground could possibly form a correct and just idea of what was passing". He cites this as one explanation of the varying accounts and contradictory statements.

Hunt, who had himself ridden in the Wiltshire Yeomanry, thus describes the charge in his *Memoirs*: "Before the cheering was sufficiently ended to enable me to raise my voice again, the word was given, and from the left flank of the troops, the trumpeter leading the way, they charged amongst the people, sabring right and left, in all directions, sparing neither age, sex, nor rank. In this manner they cut their way up to the hustings, riding over and sabring all that could not get out of their way."

Finally, let us hear the officer speak who led the charge in person. At the Royal Birthday festivities in Manchester on the 29th of April, 1820, Colonel Hugh Birley, in replying to the toast of the Manchester and Salford Yeomanry, made a lengthy speech, in which he complained bitterly of the obloquy and outcry levelled against them, "which we should have been more or less than men not to feel". Speaking of the charge into the crowd, he said: "I observed as I approached the stage a movement in the crowd about the spot from which all accounts agree in stating that the first attack was made upon the Yeomanry. That movement appeared to be intended to throw an obstacle in the way of our advance. Up to that moment the Boroughreeve had walked by my side, but I then quickened my pace in order to prevent an interruption. There was ample space for a front of six men where-ever we passed, but I am assured by those who formed the first rank of six that they were obliged to break off into single file before they reached the stage. The mob must there-

---

47  Moiled is an archaic word for confused or agitated.

fore have closed in immediately behind the officers who led the squadron."
He goes on to speak of the Yeomanry's dash for the flags, which is mentioned
below. He does not attempt to deny that it took place; but there is no object in
quoting further from an *apologia* which at the best is a very lame affair.

The arrival of the other troops is thus described in the *Manchester
Chronicle*: "Immediately the Cheshire Yeomanry galloped on the ground;
to them succeeded the 15th Hussars, and the Royal Artillery train; while all
the various detachments of infantry also advanced". Stanley has this footnote on the infantry: "on quitting the ground I for the first time observed
that strong bodies of infantry were posted in the streets on opposite sides
of the square; their appearance might probably have increased the alarm,
and would certainly have impeded the progress of a mob wishing to retreat
in either of these directions. When I saw them they were resting on their
arms, and I believe they remained stationary, taking no part in the proceedings". In his plan Stanley[48] shows the Cheshire Yeomanry halting between
Windmill Street and the hustings, and the 15th Hussars halting in front of
Mount Street, about opposite to the present Midland Buffet. He says: "The
Manchester Yeomanry had already taken possession of the hustings when
the Cheshire Yeomanry entered on my left in excellent order, and formed
in the rear of the hustings, as well as could be expected considering the
crowds who were now pressing in all directions and filling up the space
hitherto partially occupied. The 15th Dragoons appeared nearly at the same
moment and paused rather than halted on our left and parallel to the row
of houses."

# The Manchester Yeomanry in Difficulties

WE HAVE NOW ARRIVED at the most dramatic moment in the whole story, and it may be well to review the situation before coming to the fateful decision which completed the tragedy. One troop of the Manchester and Salford Yeomanry (perhaps consisting of fifty or sixty men) was now practically enveloped in the huge crowd. So serious did Mr. Hulton consider their case to be that he stated at the Trial that he "saw what appeared to be a general resistance ... the Manchester Yeomanry he conceived to be completely defeated ... his idea of their danger arose from his seeing sticks flourished in the air as well as brickbats[49] thrown about". We have also, however, the testimony of an officer of Regulars as to the situation. Lieutenant Sir W. Jolliffe, who afterwards charged the crowd with the Hussars, says: "the Manchester Yeomanry were scattered in small groups over the greater part of the field, literally hemmed up and wedged into the mob, so that they were powerless either to make an impression or to escape; in fact, *they were in the power of those whom they were designed to overawe*; and it required only a glance to discover their helpless position and the necessity of our being brought to the rescue".

There are two points on which the evidence is hopelessly conflicting: the first is the question of the use of missiles by the crowd. There is no method of discussing the question except that of quoting the various testimonies. Mr. Hulton stated that his reason for thinking the Yeomanry in danger was that he saw sticks flourished in the air and brickbats thrown about, and "that he saw what appeared to be a general resistance". He afterwards said at the Trial: "I have not stated that bricks and stones were levelled at the Yeomanry and I can't swear it. They were thrown in defiance of the military." Mr. Stanley, on the other hand, says: "I saw nothing that gave me an idea of resistance, except in one or two spots where they showed some disinclination to abandon their banners; these impulses, however, were but momentary; their sticks, as far as came under my observation, were ordinary walking sticks. I have heard from the most respectable authority that the cavalry were assailed by stones during the short time they halted previous to their charge. I do not wish to contradict positive assertions. What a

---

49 A piece of brick used as a missile. The 'bat' part comes from the Old English for a cudgel or club.

person sees must be true. My evidence on that point can only be negative. I certainly saw nothing of the sort, and my eyes were fixed most steadily upon them, and I think that I must have seen any stone larger than a pebble at the short distance at which I stood and with the commanding view I had. *I indeed saw no missile weapons used throughout the whole transaction*; but, as I have before stated, the dust at the hustings soon partially obscured everything that took place near that particular spot, but no doubt the people defended themselves to the best of their power, as it was absolutely impossible for them to get away and give the cavalry a clear passage till the outer part of the mob had fallen back."

Bamford admits that when a number of Middleton people, who were pressed by the Yeomanry, retreated to the timber lying in front of the Friends' Meeting House, they "defended themselves with stones which they found there," and he tells of a young married woman who defended herself here for some time, and at length, being herself wounded, threw "a fragment of a brick" with the result that one of the Yeomanry was "unhorsed and dangerously wounded". This incident is confirmed by the report in the *Chronicle*, which runs: "Another Yeomanry man was unhorsed at the same moment, and his life with difficulty saved. This was near the Quakers' meeting-house, where a furious battle raged." The same paper mentions "large stones". At the Trials it was stated in defence of the magistrates that previous to the meeting the town surveyor had carefully cleared the ground of all stones, but that after it was over a cartload of stones and bricks was picked up.

Mr. Tyas, the reporter for *The Times*, says emphatically that when the Yeomanry rode into the crowd "not a brickbat was thrown at them, not a pistol was fired—during this period all was quiet and orderly, as if the cavalry had been the friends of the multitude and had marched as such into the midst of them. As soon as Hunt and Johnson had jumped from the waggon, a cry was made by the cavalry: 'Have at their flags!' In consequence, they immediately dashed, not only at the flags that were in the waggon, but those which were posted among the crowd, cutting most indiscriminately to the right and left in order to get at them. This set the people running in all directions, and *it was not until this act had been committed that any brickbats were hurled at the military*. From that moment the Manchester Yeomanry lost all command of their temper." One of those who held on to his banner till it was struck from his hand, and his shoulder was divided by one of the Manchester Yeomanry (whom he recognised) was the Middleton journeyman,[50] Thomas Redford. Three years later, in 1822, this man sued

---

50  A skilled worker who was paid a day rate for his work.

members of the Manchester Yeomanry for assault at a famous trial which took place at Lancaster.[51]

After the lapse of a century, perhaps we may, while trying to take an impartial view, agree with what Mr. Hobhouse said on this subject in the House of Commons in May, 1821, in supporting Sir Francis Burdett's motion for an inquiry: He "defied proof that the people began it. When once they were attacked, what could you expect? Were people in the quiet exercise of one of their most undoubted privileges to be unresistingly bayonetted, sabred, trampled underfoot, without raising a hand, or (if the noble lord would allow) without putting their hands in their pockets for the stones they had brought with them? The Rev. Mr. Stanley, who watched the proceedings from a room above the magistrates, saw no stones or sticks used." The mention of pockets is a reference to a report that some of the crowd wore smocks with large pockets, in which they brought stones to the meeting.

The second question that gave rise to much discussion at the Trials and elsewhere was whether the Riot Act was read before the second body of troops was directed to charge the crowd. It was emphatically stated at the Trial that the Act was read distinctly twice: once from the magistrates' window. Mr. Stanley, who stood at the window immediately above the magistrates, was closely questioned on this point at the Trial in 1822. He said: "I neither heard it read nor saw it read". Similar testimony was given by Mr. McKennell, who stood on the steps of Mr. Buxton's house throughout the proceedings. Further discussion of this point is unnecessary because it seems to be fairly generally admitted that if the Riot Act was read (as it may well have been in a perfunctory way) no one whom it concerned had any knowledge of the fact; and supposing again that it was read, the time that elapsed between the reading of the Act and the charge of the troops was much less than that prescribed by the Act itself.

---

51  Redford failed in his attempt to be compensated for his injuries. The court was unsympathetic and in his summing up the judge said: "We have heard it stated that 14 persons were killed, and 600 wounded. I have no doubt the learned Counsel has been told that; but I do not wish that Counsel would recollect that what comes from them comes with great authority, and has great influence on the public mind. I wish, therefore, that they would not, without evidence, state any such facts. There is not a *scintilla* of proof of any such thing; in the contrary, all the witnesses say they saw no person whatever killed."

# The Fateful Decision. The Hussars Ordered to Charge

W E NOW RETURN TO the scene in St. Peter's fields at the moment when the new troops arrived. Lieut.-Colonel L'Estrange, who was in command of the whole, and who had come round into Windmill Street with the 15th Hussars and the Cheshire Yeomanry, halted both, rode up to the house where the magistrates were assembled, and, looking up at the window at which Mr. Hulton (their chairman) was standing, said: "What am I to do?" Hulton admitted afterwards at the Trial that he did not consult his brother magistrates before replying. "There was not time," he said, "for me to consult my brother magistrates as to sending in more military, but they were with me at the window, and I should certainly conceive they heard me. I did not take the responsibility on myself. They at that moment were expressing fear themselves."

Mr. Hulton's fateful reply to Lieut.-Colonel L'Estrange (he repeated it over and over again at the Trials) was as follows: "Good God, sir! don't you see they are attacking the Yeomanry? Disperse the meeting."

The scene that followed these words was one that sent a thrill of horror through the whole country—the report of it reached the poet Shelley in Italy, and he says:—

> As I lay asleep in Italy
> There came a Voice from over the Sea,
> And with great power it forth led me
> To walk in the visions of Poesy

and he wrote his "Mask of Anarchy". Within ten minutes from the time those words were uttered, those who looked down on St. Peter's fields saw an open space, strewn with human beings, some dead, many wounded, numbers of them heaped one upon the other—and a group of horsemen loosening their saddle-girths, arranging their accoutrements, and wiping their sabres, while all round there was a flying multitude, escaping by the side streets, which were guarded by infantry, defending themselves among the timber lying near the Friends' Meeting House, and eventually making their way to the open country, through which they had marched a few hours before, with bands playing, banners flying, and girls dancing and singing, with an exultant feeling of hope that at last something was to be done for their suffering humanity.

We have many pictures of the scene. Stanley says: "The 15th Dragoons pressed forward, crossing the line of constables, which opened to let them through, and bent their course towards the Manchester Yeomanry. The people were now in a state of utter rout and confusion, leaving the ground strewn with hats and shoes, and hundreds were thrown down in the attempt to escape. The cavalry were hurrying about in all directions completing the work of dispersion, which was effected in so short a time as to appear as if done by magic. During the whole of this confusion, heightened at its close by the rattle of some artillery crossing the square, shrieks were heard in all directions, and as the crowd of people dispersed, the effects of the conflict became visible. Some were seen bleeding on the ground, unable to rise; others, less seriously injured, but faint with the loss of blood, were retiring slowly, or leaning upon others for support. The whole of this extraordinary scene was the work of a few minutes." Bamford speaks of "several mounds of human beings remaining where they had fallen, crushed down and smothered". This is fully corroborated by Sir W. Jolliffe, the Lieutenant of the Hussars already quoted, who says: "People, yeomen, and constables, in their confused attempts to escape, ran one over the other, so that by the time we had arrived at the end of the field, the fugitives were literally piled up to a considerable elevation above the level of the field". Wheeler's *Manchester Chronicle*, the principal Tory organ, had the following description on the Saturday following the event:—

"A scene of confusion and terror now existed which defies description. The multitude pressed one another down, and in many places they lay in masses, piled body upon body. The cries and mingled shouts with the galloping of the horses were shocking. Many of the most respectable gentlemen of the town were thrown down, ridden over and trampled upon. One special constable was killed on the spot; another was borne home dreadfully hurt. The whole of this serious affray lasted not many minutes. The ground was cleared as if by magic."

Bamford's account runs: "On the breaking of the crowd the yeomanry wheeled, and dashing wherever there was an opening, they followed, pressing and wounding. Many females and striplings appeared as the crowd opened; their cries were piteous and heartrending. In ten minutes from the commencement of the havoc, the field was an open and almost deserted space." Mr. J.B. Smith's report of what he saw from the window in Mount Street corresponds.

Exactly how, we may be inclined to ask, was the charge of the Hussars made? Lieutenant Jolliffe, who took part in it, shall answer the question. We must premise, however, that he has his cardinal points wrong. For "southwest" we must read "south-east," and for "south" we must read "east". There is no doubt that the Hussars lined up in Mount Street, and swept the square from Mount Street to Deansgate. This is clear, not only from Stanley's plan, but also from Jolliffe's own statement that his troopers found themselves in Byrom Street after crossing the square. He writes: "Some one who had been sent from the place of meeting to bring us, led the way through a number of narrow streets by a circuitous route to (what I will call) the south-west corner of St. Peter's fields. We advanced along the south side of this space of ground, without a halt or pause even; the words 'Front!' and 'Forward!' were given, and the trumpet sounded the charge, at the very moment the threes wheeled up. When fronted, our line extended quite across the ground, which in all parts was so filled with people that their hats seemed to touch." When the square was cleared, Lieutenant Jolliffe was sent by his commander to find a trumpeter, in order that he might sound the "Rally" or "Retreat". "This sent me down the street I had first been in [i.e. Byrom Street, or possibly St. John Street] after the pursuing men of my troop."

There are four other points touched upon in Lieutenant Jolliffe's narrative, which should not be omitted if the story is to be complete. We have already mentioned the loose baulks of timber that lay scattered about to the south of the Friends' Meeting House. These "timber-trees," as he calls them, "could not be distinguished when the mob covered them, and they caused bad falls to one officer's horse and to many of the troopers" of the Hussars. Jolliffe himself went to the assistance of "a private of the regiment whose horse had fallen over a piece of timber nearly in the middle of the square, and who was most seriously injured".

Lieutenant Jolliffe's account of the fight near the Friends' Meeting House, also mentioned above, runs thus: "The mob had taken possession of various buildings, particularly of a Quakers' chapel and burial-ground enclosed with a wall. This they occupied for some little time, and in attempting to displace them some of the men and horses were struck with stones and brickbats. Seeing a sort of fighting going on, I went in that direction. At the very moment I reached the Quakers' Meeting House, I saw a farrier of the 15th ride at a small door in the outer wall, and to my surprise his horse struck it with such force that it flew open. Two or three hussars then rode in, and the place was immediately in their possession."

The statement in the *Chronicle* on the following Saturday to the effect that "one of the Yeomanry leaped his horse over the wall after a Reformer" would seem to be apocryphal, as the plan produced at the Trial showed that there was a drop of 10 feet on one side. I have to thank the authorities who have charge of the archives at the Friends' Meeting House for their courtesy in acceding to my request that the Records and Minute Books for August, 1819, should be examined. They could find no mention whatever of Peterloo.

Lieutenant Jolliffe also clears up the following reference in Stanley's account. Stanley says: "I saw no firearms, but distinctly heard four or five shots towards the close of the business on the opposite side of the square, beyond the hustings, but no one could inform me by whom they were fired". Jolliffe tells of a pistol fired from a window; and a footnote by Captain Smyth of the Cheshire Yeomanry refers to some men on the roof of a house with a gun. "The 88th fired a shot or two over the roof and cleared the spot."

Lastly, the question arises: What use was made of the Cheshire Yeomanry when they arrived in St. Peter's fields? Stanley, who shows them halting between the hustings and Windmill Street, adds this note to his plan: "My attention was so much taken up with the proceedings of the Manchester Yeomanry, etc., and the dispersion in front of the hustings, that I cannot speak accurately as to their subsequent movements". It is clear that they cannot have charged the crowd from that point. They would have been riding at right angles to the charge of the Hussars. The Centenary Volume of the Cheshire Yeomanry throws no light on the matter. The most detailed contemporary plan shows Yeomanry and foot-soldiers at different points "intercepting and cutting at fugitives". Lieutenant Jolliffe, speaking of the Cheshire Yeomanry and the 31st Infantry, says: "the whole remained formed up till our squadrons had fallen in again". Captain Smyth, who led one of the troops of the Cheshire Yeomanry, says (in a footnote to Jolliffe's account): "The Yeomanry and Infantry stationed at the four corners opened to allow the multitude to escape". We are therefore driven to the conclusion that l'Estrange held the Cheshire Yeomanry in reserve while the Hussars made their charge.

We have at least two testimonies as to the appearance of the fugitives as they streamed into the open country. Mr. Prentice had left the crowd to go to his home in Salford just as Hunt had mounted the hustings. "I had not been at home more than a quarter of an hour," he says, "when a wailing sound was heard from the main street, and rushing out, I saw people running in the direction of Pendleton, their faces pale as death, and some with blood trickling down their cheeks. It was with difficulty I could get anyone to stop and tell me what had happened. The unarmed multitude, men, women and children, had been attacked with murderous results by the military." Mr. William Royle, in his *History of Rusholme*, published in 1914, says: "I remember my father telling me that on the day of the Peterloo massacre in 1819 he was standing at the corner of Norman Road, and saw crowds of people coming from Manchester, many with marks of blood upon them received in that murderous affray".

Meanwhile, Hunt, who was brutally maltreated after his arrest, had been hurried with the other prisoners to the New Bailey in Salford. The military and special constables patrolled the streets. Apparently the temper of the crowd had been roused to a dangerous pitch. Stanley, who praises the quiet demeanour of the people before the event, says: "At the conclusion of the business I found them in a very different state of feeling. I heard repeated vows of revenge. 'You took us unprepared, we were unarmed to-day, and it is your day, but when we meet again the day shall be ours.'" Bamford, who led the remnant of his contingent into Middleton with a band and one remaining banner, corroborates this: "All the working people of Manchester I found athirst for revenge"; the Middleton folk "brooding over a spirit of vengeance towards the authors of our humiliation and our wrong". The centre of disorder seems to have been at New Cross. The Riot Act was read at this place between seven and eight, and a number of people were wounded, one fatally, by shots from the military.

But in these days of hospitals and Red Cross Societies our thoughts inevitably follow the wounded as they made their way painfully homewards. Thousands of those at the meeting had come from as far as Bury, and had to walk back. The Committee that was afterwards formed for their relief drew up a list of authenticated cases, from which it appears that we may safely say that eleven were killed and between 500 and 600 more or less seriously injured. The subscriptions to the relief fund amounted to over £3000. As examples, let us follow two of the wounded to their homes on the fateful 16th of August. "It was," says Bamford, in speaking of Redford's wound, "a clean gash of about six inches in length and quite through the shoulder blade. I found Redford's mother bathing it. She yearned and wept afresh when she saw the severed bone gaping in the wound. She asked who did it, and Tom mentioned a person; he said he knew him well, and she, sobbing, said she also knew him and his father and mother before him." There is another point to remember. Reliable authorities assure us that in many cases the wounded dare not apply for proper treatment, for fear of losing employment by being branded as Reformers. We have already mentioned that Redford's case was the subject of a test trial three years later, when he sued the yeomanry for "unlawful cutting and wounding," but the Jury found for the defendants in a few minutes. The other case, a much more painful one, and yet one that must be typical of many, was that of an Oldham youth named John Lees, who had fought at Waterloo, who came home with external and internal injuries to which he succumbed after the most excruciating suffering. Those who wish may read all the harrowing details of this most painful case in the Report of the Inquest, which after dragging on for a number of months was eventually quashed by a legal quibble.

As he rode back across the square, Lieutenant Jolliffe had noticed, lying here and there, "the unfortunates who were too much injured to move away, and the sight was rendered more distressing by observing some women among the sufferers". On the following afternoon he "visited the Infirmary in company with some military medical officers. I saw there from

HENRY HUNT'S BIRTHPLACE ON SALISBURY PLAIN.

THE PRISON CELLS IN LANCASTER CASTLE WHERE HENRY HUNT AND SAMUEL
BAMFORD WERE CONFINED AFTER PETERLOO.

twelve to twenty cases of sabre-wounds, and among these two women who appeared not likely to recover. … One man was in a dying state from a gun-shot wound in the head; another had had his leg amputated; both these casualties arose from the firing of the 88th the night before. Two or three were reported dead, one of them a constable killed in St. Peter's fields, but I saw none of the bodies."

It was not till half-past ten on Wednesday morning that the Prince Regent's Cheshire Yeomanry, in their blue jackets, with silver-braid ornament, scarlet cuffs and collar, and plated buttons—having spent one night patrolling the town, and another "lying at their horses' heads in St. Peter's fields"—mounted and rode away home, where they were warmly welcomed. Many of them had made their wills before they had set out for Manchester two days earlier, with serious misgivings.

Such is the story of Peterloo. "After Peterloo" is a story in itself. Into the details of that story—the meeting held at the Star Inn a few days later, to vote the thanks of the "Inhabitants of Manchester" to the Magistrates and the Military—the indignant "Declaration and Protest," bearing some 5000 signatures, which followed immediately, and showed incontestably that that meeting was private and quite unrepresentative—Mr. Francis Phillips's ably written "Exposure of the Calumnies circulated against the Magistrates and the Yeomanry"—Mr. John Edward Taylor's spirited "Reply" to this—the Thanks of the Prince Regent to the Magistrates and the Military, sent at the instigation of Lord Sidmouth, the Home Secretary, whose first remark on hearing of the tragedy was that he "trusted the proceedings at Manchester would prove a salutary lesson to modern reformers"—the "Papers relative to the internal state of the country" presented to Parliament in the autumn, containing the correspondence between the Magistrates and the Home Office—Mr. J.E. Taylor's "Notes and Observations" on these, which Sir A.W. Ward has pronounced to be "the chief monument of his literary powers and political principles"—the storm of indignation that arose in Great Britain and Ireland—the great meetings held in London and the Provinces to demand inquiry (for summoning one of which Earl Fitzwilliam was immediately removed from the Lord-Lieutenancy of the West Riding, "the Prince Regent[52] having no further occasion for his services")—the deter-

---

52  King George III was ill and Parliament had arranged for the Prince of Wales (the future George IV) to be appointed Regent in 1811. George had fewer powers than his father and was content to let his ministers look after government busi-

mination of ministers, nevertheless, to burke[53] inquiry, which led to protests on all hands (Earl Grosvenor, e.g. sent £50 to the Relief Fund, "not as a friend of Universal Suffrage," but as protesting against the refusal to allow investigation; while Lord Carlisle, in a confidential letter, since made public by the Historical Documents Commission, characterised the conduct of the Government in this particular matter as "marked by downright insanity," though he afterwards supported the third reading of their Seditious Meetings Bill)—the protest presented to the Prince Regent by the Lord Mayor, Aldermen, and Commons of the City of London—the triumphal procession of Mr. Hunt from Lancaster to Manchester, and his reception by enormous crowds in London—the interminable discussions as to the legality of the meeting, and the right of the magistrates to interfere—the careful investigation by the Relief Committee of some 600 cases of those killed and wounded in the fray—the harrowing details (reported by Taylor himself) revealed at the Inquest at Oldham, which, after dragging on for months, was quashed by the Court of King's Bench, because, forsooth, the Coroner and the Jury had not viewed the body at the same time—the sternly repressive policy adopted by the Government, culminating in the famous Six Acts,[54] in introducing which Lord Castlereagh admitted that the Manchester meeting was not contrary to law, an admission which Mr. Hobhouse immediately seized upon as the text for his masterly "Letter to Lord Viscount Castlereagh"—the long debates in Parliament year after

ness. It was at this time that the principle was established that the prime minister was the person supported by a majority in the House of Commons, whether the king favoured him or not.

53 An archaic word meaning to suppress. It originally came from William Burke who, together with William Hare, used to acquire bodies for Edinburgh anatomy schools. In order to increase their "stock", Burke and Hare, in 1827, would lure victims to a boarding house and suffocate or strangle them. At first, burke came to mean death by suffocation or strangulation and eventually for any suppression.

54 This legislation was introduced after the massacre and was intended to suppress meetings and opportunities for Radical reform. The six acts were: Training Prevention Act (military training was to be done only by municipal bodies, etc.); Seizure of Arms Act (allowed magistrates to search for and seize weapons); Misdemeanours Act (reduced bail and increased the speed of trials); Seditious Meetings Act (prohibited meetings of more than 50 people without permission); Blasphemous and Seditious Libels Act (or Criminal Libel Act) (increased sentences for authors of radical literature); and Newspaper and Stamp Duties Act (extended and increased taxes to cover publications which had previously avoided duty by publishing opinion and not news).

THE PETERLOO MEDAL. NOTE THE WOMEN AND CHILDREN, AND THE CAP OF
LIBERTY HELD ALOFT IN THE CENTRE.

year—the fining and imprisonment of Sir Francis Burdett for too severely censuring the action of the Government—the tramp of the Manchester
Reformers over the Pennines to take their trial at York Assizes, in the course
of which "the ascent of Blackstone Edge tried the marching powers of the
women"—the long days of the Trial itself—the subtle summing-up of the
Judge—the verdict against the leading Reformers, as guilty of "assembling
with unlawful banners an unlawful assembly, for the purpose of moving
and inciting the liege subjects of our sovereign lord the King to contempt
and hatred of the Government and Constitution of the Realm, as by law
established"—the quashed appeal—the subsequent proceedings in the
Court of King's Bench, when sentence was pronounced, Hunt afterwards
serving two and a half years in Ilminster jail, Bamford, Johnson, and Healey
one year at Lincoln—the test trial at Lancaster three years after Peterloo,
when Thomas Redford sued the Manchester Yeomanry for "unlawful cutting and wounding," and the jury found for the defendants in six minutes—
and finally, the periodical discussion of all these things in the press—into
the details of these matters we do not enter here.

St. Peter's fields have long ago become part of the great city, the chief
centre of its entertainments, strangely enough, and the site of the Battle for
Free Trade; the Friends' Meeting House has been rebuilt, and the oak trees
have disappeared; the site of Cooper's cottage and garden is now covered
by "one of the finest hotels in Europe"; the exigencies of modern traffic have
swept away the dark pile of St. Peter's church, whose grimy clock was once
such a familiar object; but as we stand in front of the Central Station to-
day, the Halls of Pleasure disappear, and the picture that haunts us is that
of a stricken field, the victims lying in heaps—"some still groaning, others
with staring eyes, gasping for breath, others will never breathe more; all
silent, save for those low sounds, and the occasional snorting and pawing
of steeds". It all seems so unfair. They were *inarticulate*. They had come,
with all the hilarity of a general holiday, to ask that they might have a Voice.
They were met by the bungling of incompetent authorities, behind whom
loomed the great, strong, repressive Government, saying: "I am God,
and King, and Law," backed by a House of Commons that was hopelessly
unrepresentative.

Yet their blood, as has been well said, proved in the end to be the seed
of some of our most cherished liberties. "The Manchester massacre," wrote
Harriet Martineau,[55] speaking, of course, as a Radical herself, "was at once
felt on all hands to have made an epoch in the history of the contest with

---

55 Harriet Martineau (1802–76) was an English writer and social theorist.

Radicalism". Parliamentary Representation came, and Local Government based on the Suffrage soon followed, the antiquated manorial Court giving place eventually to the Manchester Corporation. In his famous pamphlet entitled "Incorporate your Borough," issued to the people of Manchester less than twenty years later, in 1838, Richard Cobden[56] wrote: "Peterloo could never have happened if the Borough had been incorporated. Why? Because the magistrates of Lancashire and Cheshire, who entered the town and sat at the Star Inn to take command of the police, and order the soldiers to cut down and trample upon unarmed crowds, would have no more jurisdiction over Manchester than Constantinople"; and in her *History of the Thirty Years' Peace*, from which we have already quoted, Harriet Martineau describes Peterloo as "the great event of the year, and the most memorable incident in the history of the popular movements of the time".

The author[57] of "Childe Harold"[58] speaks of the "red rain" that fell at Waterloo, and "made the harvest grow" on the fields of Belgium. Perhaps we may, not inappropriately, borrow his figure, and say that the red rain that fell at Peterloo, four years later, has helped to ripen another harvest—the harvest of Freedom.

---

56 Richard Cobden (1804–65) was a Radical politician who campaigned for free trade and to end the Corn Laws.

57 Lord Byron (1788–1824) who has been described a leading Romantic poet and also as "mad, bad, and dangerous to know".

58 *Childe Harold's Pilgrimage* is a book-length poem, published between 1812 and 1818.

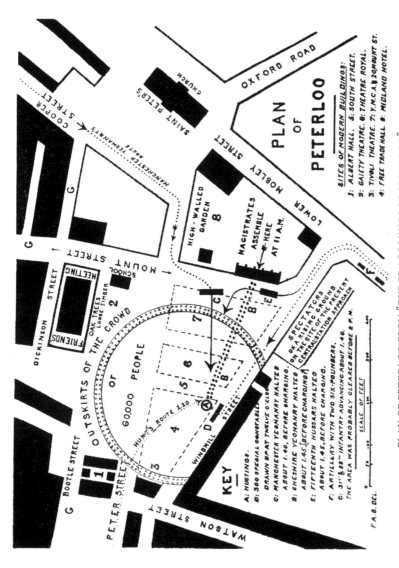

PLAN OF PETERLOO FROM "THREE ACCOUNTS OF PETERLOO".

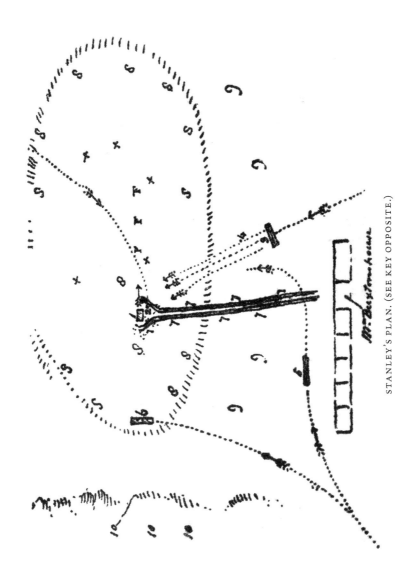

STANLEY'S PLAN. (SEE KEY OPPOSITE.)

# The key to Stanley's plan

1. The hustings. The arrow shows the direction in which the orators addressed the mob, the great majority being in front: F, F, F.

2. The Barouche [four-wheeled horse-drawn carriage] in which Hunt arrived, the line from it showing its entrance and approach.

3. The spot on which the Manchester Yeomanry Cavalry halted previous to their charge; the dotted lines in front showing the direction of their charge on attacking the hustings.

4. On this spot the woman alluded to in the account was wounded and remained apparently dead, till removed at the conclusion of the business.

5. Here the 15th Dragoons paused for a few moments before they proceeded in the direction marked by the dotted line.

6. The Cheshire Cavalry; my attention was so much taken up with the proceedings of the Manchester Yeomanry Cavalry, etc., and the dispersion in front of the hustings, that I cannot speak accurately as to their subsequent movements.

7,7,7. The band of special constables, apparently surrounding the hustings.

8,8,8. The mob in dense mass; their banners displayed in different parts, as at x, x.

9,9,9. A space comparatively vacant; partially occupied by stragglers; the mob condensing near the hustings for the purpose of seeing and hearing.

10,10,10. Raised ground on which many spectators had taken a position; a commotion amongst them first announced the approach of the cavalry; their elevated situation commanding a more extensive view.

PERCY BYSSHE SHELLEY 1792–1822

# The Mask of Anarchy

## *Written on the occasion of the massacre at Manchester*

## by Percy Bysshe Shelley

As I lay asleep in Italy[1]
There came a voice from over the Sea,
And with great power it forth led me
To walk in the visions of Poesy.[2]

I met Murder on the way—
He had a mask like Castlereagh[3]—
Very smooth he looked, yet grim;
Seven blood-hounds followed him:

All were fat; and well they might
Be in admirable plight,
For one by one, and two by two,
He tossed them human hearts to chew
Which from his wide cloak he drew.

Next came Fraud, and he had on,
Like Lord Eldon,[4] an ermined gown;
His big tears, for he wept well,
Turned to mill-stones as they fell.

---

1 Shelley was living in Italy at the time with his second wife Mary (*née* Godwin).

2 An archaic word for poetry.

3 Viscount Castlereagh, an Anglo-Irish politician, was Leader of the House of Commons and defended his government's actions.

4 Lord Eldon was the lord chancellor – responsible for the law courts. As a judge he supposedly wept as he passed his judgments. He had refused Shelley custody of his own children after Shelley's first wife's suicide.

And the little children, who
Round his feet played to and fro,
Thinking every tear a gem,
Had their brains knocked out by them.

Clothed with the Bible, as with light,
And the shadows of the night,
Like Sidmouth,[5] next, Hypocrisy
On a crocodile[6] rode by.

And many more Destructions played
In this ghastly masquerade,
All disguised, even to the eyes,
Like Bishops, lawyers, peers, and spies.

Last came Anarchy:[7] he rode
On a white horse, splashed with blood;
He was pale even to the lips,
Like Death in the Apocalypse.

And he wore a kingly crown;
And in his grasp a sceptre shone;
On his brow this mark I saw—
'I AM GOD, AND KING, AND LAW!'

With a pace stately and fast,
Over English land he passed,
Trampling to a mire of blood
The adoring multitude.

---

5 Viscount Sidmouth was home secretary and had suspended habeus corpus
in 1817 as he was of the opinion that there was "a traitorous conspiracy ... for the
purpose of overthrowing ... the established government".

6 There is ancient belief that crocodiles shed tears while consuming their prey.

7 Anarchy becomes the fourth horseman of the Apocalypse along with
Castlereagh, Eldon and Sidmouth.

And with a mighty troop around
With their trampling shook the ground,
Waving each a bloody sword,
For the service of their Lord.

And with glorious triumph they
Rode through England proud and gay,
Drunk as with intoxication
Of the wine of desolation.

O'er fields and towns, from sea to sea,
Passed the Pageant swift and free,
Tearing up, and trampling down;
Till they came to London town.

And each dweller, panic-stricken,
Felt his heart with terror sicken
Hearing the tempestuous cry
Of the triumph of Anarchy.

For from pomp to meet him came,
Clothed in arms like blood and flame,
The hired murderers, who did sing
'Thou art God, and Law, and King.

'We have waited weak and lone
For thy coming, Mighty One!
Our purses are empty, our swords are cold,
Give us glory, and blood, and gold.'

Lawyers and priests a motley crowd,
To the earth their pale brows bowed;
Like a bad prayer not over loud,
Whispering—'Thou art Law and God.'—

Then all cried with one accord,
'Thou art King, and God, and Lord;
Anarchy, to thee we bow,
Be thy name made holy now!'

And Anarchy, the Skeleton,[8]
Bowed and grinned to every one,
As well as if his education
Had cost ten millions to the nation.[9]

For he knew the Palaces
Of our Kings were rightly his;
His the sceptre, crown, and globe,
And the gold-inwoven robe.

So he sent his slaves before
To seize upon the Bank and Tower,[10]
And was proceeding with intent
To meet his pensioned Parliament[11]

When one fled past, a maniac maid,
And her name was Hope, she said:
But she looked more like Despair,
And she cried out in the air:

'My father Time is weak and grey
With waiting for a better day;
See how idiot-like he stands,
Fumbling with his palsied hands!

'He has had child after child,
And the dust of death is piled
Over every one but me—
Misery, oh, Misery!'

8  Death, the final horseman of the Apocalypse is often depicted as a skeleton.

9  A reference to the national debt. Poorer people suffered disproportionately from taxes enacted to reduce the debt accrued during the American and Napoleonic Wars.

10  The Bank of England and the Tower of London.

11  Parliamentarians, like today's, had excessive pensions.

Then she lay down in the street,
Right before the horses feet,
Expecting, with a patient eye,
Murder, Fraud, and Anarchy.

When between her and her foes
A mist, a light, an image rose.
Small at first, and weak, and frail
Like the vapour of a vale:

Till as clouds grow on the blast,
Like tower-crowned giants striding fast,
And glare with lightnings as they fly,
And speak in thunder to the sky.

It grew—a Shape arrayed in mail
Brighter than the viper's scale,
And upborne on wings whose grain
Was as the light of sunny rain.

On its helm, seen far away,
A planet, like the Morning's, lay;
And those plumes its light rained through
Like a shower of crimson dew.

With step as soft as wind it passed
O'er the heads of men—so fast
That they knew the presence there,
And looked,—but all was empty air.

As flowers beneath May's footstep waken,
As stars from Night's loose hair are shaken,
As waves arise when loud winds call,
Thoughts sprung where'er that step did fall.

And the prostrate multitude
Looked—and ankle-deep in blood,
Hope, that maiden most serene,
Was walking with a quiet mien:

And Anarchy, the ghastly birth,
Lay dead Earth upon the Earth;
The Horse of Death tameless as wind
Fled, and with his hoofs did grind
To dust the murderers thronged behind.

A rushing light of clouds and splendour,
A sense awakening and yet tender
Was heard and felt—and at its close
These words of joy and fear arose

As if their own indignant Earth
Which gave the sons of England birth
Had felt their blood upon her brow,
And shuddering with a mother's throe

Had turned every drop of blood
By which her face had been bedewed
To an accent unwithstood,—
As if her heart cried out aloud:

'Men of England, heirs of Glory,
Heroes of unwritten story,
Nurslings of one mighty Mother,
Hopes of her, and one another;

'Rise like Lions after slumber
In unvanquishable number.
Shake your chains to Earth like dew
Which in sleep had fallen on you—
Ye are many—they are few.

'What is Freedom?—ye can tell
That which slavery is, too well—
For its very name has grown
To an echo of your own.

''Tis to work and have such pay
As just keeps life from day to day
In your limbs, as in a cell
For the tyrants' use to dwell,

'So that ye for them are made
Loom, and plough, and sword, and spade,
With or without your own will bent
To their defence and nourishment.

' 'Tis to see your children weak
With their mothers pine and peak,
When the winter winds are bleak,—
They are dying whilst I speak.

' 'Tis to hunger for such diet
As the rich man in his riot
Casts to the fat dogs that lie
Surfeiting beneath his eye;

' 'Tis to let the Ghost of Gold
Take from Toil a thousandfold
More than e'er its substance could
In the tyrannies of old.

'Paper coin—that forgery[12]
Of the title-deeds, which ye
Hold to something from the worth
Of the inheritance of Earth.

' 'Tis to be a slave in soul
And to hold no strong control
Over your own wills, but be
All that others make of ye.

'And at length when ye complain
With a murmur weak and vain
'Tis to see the Tyrant's crew
Ride over your wives and you—
Blood is on the grass like dew.

---

12 Shelley distrusted the motives behind the introduction of banknotes.

'Then it is to feel revenge
Fiercely thirsting to exchange
Blood for blood—and wrong for wrong—
Do not thus when ye are strong.

'Birds find rest, in narrow nest
When weary of their wingèd quest;
Beasts find fare, in woody lair
When storm and snow are in the air.

'Horses, oxen, have a home,
When from daily toil they come;
Household dogs, when the wind roars,
Find a home within warm doors.'

'Asses, swine, have litter spread
And with fitting food are fed;
All things have a home but one—
Thou, Oh, Englishman, hast none!

'This is Slavery—savage men,
Or wild beasts within a den
Would endure not as ye do—
But such ills they never knew.

'What art thou, Freedom? O! could slaves
Answer from their living graves
This demand—tyrants would flee
Like a dream's imagery:

'Thou are not, as impostors say,
A shadow soon to pass away,
A superstition, and a name
Echoing from the cave of Fame.

'For the labourer thou art bread,
And a comely table spread
From his daily labour come
In a neat and happy home.

'Thou art clothes, and fire, and food
For the trampled multitude—
No—in countries that are free
Such starvation cannot be
As in England now we see.

'To the rich thou art a check,
When his foot is on the neck
Of his victim, thou dost make
That he treads upon a snake.

'Thou art Justice—ne'er for gold
May thy righteous laws be sold
As laws are in England—thou
Shield'st alike both high and low.

'Thou art Wisdom—Freemen never
Dream that God will damn for ever
All who think those things untrue
Of which Priests make such ado.

'Thou art Peace—never by thee
Would blood and treasure wasted be
As tyrants wasted them, when all
Leagued to quench thy flame in Gaul.

'What if English toil and blood
Was poured forth, even as a flood?
It availed, Oh, Liberty.
To dim, but not extinguish thee.

'Thou art Love—the rich have kissed
Thy feet, and like him following Christ,
Give their substance to the free
And through the rough world follow thee,

'Or turn their wealth to arms, and make
War for thy belovèd sake
On wealth, and war, and fraud—whence they
Drew the power which is their prey.

'Science, Poetry, and Thought
Are thy lamps; they make the lot
Of the dwellers in a cot
So serene, they curse it not.

'Spirit, Patience, Gentleness,
All that can adorn and bless
Art thou—let deeds, not words, express
Thine exceeding loveliness.

'Let a great Assembly be
Of the fearless and the free
On some spot of English ground
Where the plains stretch wide around.

'Let the blue sky overhead,
The green Earth on which ye tread,
All that must eternal be
Witness the solemnity.

'From the corners uttermost
Of the bounds of English coast;
From every hut, village, and town
Where those who live and suffer moan
For others' misery or their own,

'From the workhouse and the prison
Where pale as corpses newly risen,
Women, children, young and old
Groan for pain, and weep for cold—

'From the haunts of daily life
Where is waged the daily strife
With common wants and common cares
Which sows the human heart with tares—

'Lastly from the palaces
Where the murmur of distress
Echoes, like the distant sound
Of a wind alive around

'Those prison halls of wealth and fashion.
Where some few feel such compassion
For those who groan, and toil, and wail
As must make their brethren pale —

'Ye who suffer woes untold,
Or to feel, or to behold
Your lost country bought and sold
With a price of blood and gold —

'Let a vast assembly be,
And with great solemnity
Declare with measured words that ye
Are, as God has made ye, free —

'Be your strong and simple words
Keen to wound as sharpened swords,
And wide as targes[13] let them be,
With their shade to cover ye.

'Let the tyrants pour around
With a quick and startling sound,
Like the loosening of a sea,
Troops of armed emblazonry.

'Let the charged artillery drive
Till the dead air seems alive
With the clash of clanging wheels,
And the tramp of horses' heels.

'Let the fixèd bayonet
Gleam with sharp desire to wet
Its bright point in English blood
Looking keen as one for food.

13 Shields.

'Let the horsemen's scimitars
Wheel and flash, like sphereless stars
Thirsting to eclipse their burning
In a sea of death and mourning.

'Stand ye calm and resolute,
Like a forest close and mute,
With folded arms and looks which are
Weapons of unvanquished war,

'And let Panic, who outspeeds
The career of armèd steeds
Pass, a disregarded shade
Through your phalanx undismayed.

'Let the laws of your own land,
Good or ill, between ye stand
Hand to hand, and foot to foot,
Arbiters of the dispute,

'The old laws of England—they
Whose reverend heads with age are grey,
Children of a wiser day;
And whose solemn voice must be
Thine own echo—Liberty!

'On those who first should violate
Such sacred heralds in their state
Rest the blood that must ensue,
And it will not rest on you.

'And if then the tyrants dare
Let them ride among you there,
Slash, and stab, and maim, and hew, —
What they like, that let them do.

'With folded arms and steady eyes,
And little fear, and less surprise,
Look upon them as they slay
Till their rage has died away.'

'Then they will return with shame
To the place from which they came,
And the blood thus shed will speak
In hot blushes on their cheek.

'Every woman in the land
Will point at them as they stand—
They will hardly dare to greet
Their acquaintance in the street.

'And the bold, true warriors
Who have hugged Danger in wars
Will turn to those who would be free,
Ashamed of such base company.

'And that slaughter to the Nation
Shall steam up like inspiration,
Eloquent, oracular;
A volcano heard afar.

'And these words shall then become
Like Oppression's thundered doom
Ringing through each heart and brain.
Heard again—again—again—

'Rise like Lions after slumber
In unvanquishable number—
Shake your chains to Earth like dew
Which in sleep had fallen on you—
Ye are many—they are few.'

Printed in Great
Britain
by Amazon

32293600R00041